"Closer to the Truth Than Any Fact"

"Closer to the Truth Than Any Fact"

Memoir, Memory, *and* Jim Crow

JENNIFER JENSEN WALLACH

The University of Georgia Press

Athens & London

To Suresh
who has taught me a
great deal & who has
made my U.S. history class
so much more interesting.
Best of luck in your bright
future & keep in touch!
           All best,
           Jennifer Jensen
           Wallach

© 2008 by the University of Georgia Press
Athens, Georgia 30602
All rights reserved
Set in 11/14 Adobe Garamond by BookComp, Inc.
Printed and bound by Maple-Vail
The paper in this book meets the guidelines for
permanence and durability of the Committee on
Production Guidelines for Book Longevity of the
Council on Library Resources.

Printed in the United States of America
12 11 10 09 08 C 5 4 3 2 1

Library of Congress Cataloging-in-Publication Data

Wallach, Jennifer Jensen, 1974–
Closer to the truth than any fact : memoir, memory,
and Jim Crow / Jennifer Jensen Wallach.
        p. cm.
Includes bibliographical references and index.
ISBN-13: 978-0-8203-3069-3 (hardcover : alk. paper)
ISBN-10: 0-8203-3069-8 (hardcover : alk. paper)
1. African Americans—Social conditions—Historiography.
2. African Americans—Segregation—Historiography.
3. Race discrimination—United States—Historiography.
4. Autobiography—African American authors.
5. African Americans—Biography—History and criticism.
I. Title.
E185.61.W1925 2008
305.896'073—dc22   2007039026

British Library Cataloging-in-Publication Data available

For WFP

CONTENTS

ACKNOWLEDGMENTS

I WOULD LIKE to express my affection and gratitude to the entire Department of Afro-American Studies at the University of Massachusetts; I feel fortunate to have been trained at a place where I was exposed to so many disciplinary perspectives and diverse points of view. I would particularly like to thank John Bracey for his suggestions (and lengthy "must read" lists) during the early stages of this project. I am also grateful to Bill Strickland for his support and blunt, well-reasoned advice (much of which was proffered over cosmopolitans at the Monkey Bar). I am thankful to Esther M. A. Terry not only for advising me about this book but also for teaching me much that transcends the academic realm. Steven C. Tracy gave me a crash course in literary criticism, and his careful reading of my work challenged me and saved me from more than one embarrassing mistake. I am deeply indebted to Robert Paul Wolff, who has had a transformational impact on me both as a scholar and as a human being. What would I do without his support, his guidance, and his friendship? This book could not have been written without him. Also to Manisha Sinha, Jim Smethurst, and Ernie Allen: thanks for your support and for your savvy advice about the thickets of publishing. To Andrew Rosa and Rita Reynolds, my graduate school confidants—what can I say?

This manuscript has benefited from comments by David W. Blight, whose own work has pushed me to think broadly and in interdisciplinary ways. Thanks to Jeannie M. Whayne, another role model, for her invaluable advice and support. Jennifer Ritterhouse and Steve Estes, thank you both so much for your intelligent and perceptive critiques of the manuscript. I hope each of you will recognize your imprint on the final version. Thanks to Derek Krissoff, my editor at the University of Georgia Press. I have benefited from your professionalism, your sharp intelligence, and your great sense of style. Some of the passages in this book appeared in an earlier form as "Building a Bridge of Words: The Literary Autobiography as Historical Source Material" in *Biography: An Interdisciplinary Quarterly* 29, no. 3 (Summer 2006). I would like to thank the editors for graciously allowing me to reprint some of that material here.

The following people provided me with sustenance—emotional, financial, and/or inspirational—while I was researching and writing this book: Aaron and Gemelle Jensen, Jamie Jensen, Sarah and Matt Gates, David Briggs, Jeremy Wallach, David Jensen, Jonas Hauptman, Marty Gould, Amanda Sharkey, Lindsey Swindall, John Pincince, Grimsley Graham, members of the Department of History at Stonehill College, and members of the History, Geography, and Philosophy Department at Georgia College & State University.

Finally, thanks to my mother, Carolyn S. Briggs, for pushing me toward the hardships and pleasures of the intellectual/writing life. My work has benefited tremendously from the influence of her poetic sensibilities on my more prosaic style. Special thanks to Charles Bittner for his zealous championship of me and my work and for being a tireless sounding board, editor, and companion during the latter stages of this project.

"Closer to the Truth Than Any Fact"

Autobiography and the Transformation of Historical Understanding

BECAUSE THIS IS A BOOK about life writing, I feel a certain amount of liberty to succumb to the temptation to ground this study of autobiography in an episode from my own life history. As scholars, our personal experiences imprint the work that we produce in myriad subtle and not-so-subtle ways. Scholarly work cannot ever be completely extricated from the scholars themselves. The kinds of things we write, the subjects that attract us, and the theoretical positions that we take are all related in some way to the people we are, the experiences we have had, and the things to which we have been exposed. In deliberately inserting a piece of my own autobiography into this preface, I am being unusually candid about my relationship to this text, but the connection is there whether or not I acknowledge it.[1]

The genesis of this book dates from a specific event in my childhood. My interest in life writing, specifically in how autobiography shapes our historical understanding, originated in my own encounter with a memoir written about life in the American South in the first few decades of the twentieth century. When I was twelve years old, I discovered Richard Wright's *Black Boy* (1945), his memoir about growing up in segregated Mississippi and Arkansas. I stumbled upon the book one night when I had run out of library books to read. In desperation I had begun rummaging around a neglected bookshelf—containing books acquired from yard sales and by other forms of happenstance—that had been inexplicably placed in the laundry room of our family home. I had navigated my way around piles of dirty laundry and found a perch on top of the gold-colored dryer where I could survey books on the top shelf. When I found the tattered paperback, I was intrigued by the image of a defiantly raised black fist printed on the cover.

Instinctively and immediately I knew that there was something powerful hidden behind that image.

After a quick perusal through the pages, I was hooked. The intensity of the text—Wright's story and his breathtaking use of language—was intoxicating, so overwhelming, that something about the book seemed almost taboo. Nothing had ever impacted me this way before. *Should I be reading this?* My strict, religious parents were prone to censor my reading. Being a compliant child, I had accepted their assertion that some books were suitable while others could lead to all manner of unholiness. My parents' judgments seemed arbitrary to me, and I had no means of discerning whether this book would meet their litmus test. I could not risk finding out. *At all costs, I must keep reading.* Not wanting to take any chances that this book would be deemed inappropriate reading material for a Christian young lady, I snuck it into my bedroom (a rare act of intellectual boldness on my part), and I stayed up all night reading.

This encounter with Richard Wright was a pivotal moment in my life. In an indirect way, *Black Boy* propelled me into the field of African American studies. Wright provided me with my first introduction to southern history. He tutored me about racial intimidation and violence, about grinding poverty and hopelessness, about having aspirations even in the face of chilling repression. Perhaps even more significant, Wright showed me how important (and difficult) it is to struggle against injustice. With the strength of his personality and the power of his prose, he enlisted me into the cause of attempting to understand (and thereby combat) American racism.

I read *Black Boy* actively and empathetically. I identified easily with certain aspects of Wright's experience. Because of my sheltered, fundamentalist upbringing, I knew how it felt to be intellectually stifled, to be an outcast among my peers, and to realize that my way of thinking and being was somehow outside the mainstream. However, other chapters in his life story were completely foreign to me. I was a young white girl growing up in a middle-class family in 1980s Arkansas. Although Wright, too, had spent part of his childhood in Arkansas, he lived in the biracial Delta, while I lived in the all-white hills. Wright had come of age decades earlier and was born into a caste system far more brutal and stifling than the patriarchal ordering of my religious upbringing. Nonetheless, I was seduced by the vividness of descriptions, the magnificence and forcefulness of his prose. I took the leap of faith necessary to embrace empathetically aspects of his life story that I could not find ready parallels with in my own experience. My imaginative journey through Wright's childhood left me weary and worldwise, with a deep, emotional understanding of what it might have been like to come of age during the era of segregation.

In the years since this first encounter with Wright, I have completed a doctoral degree in Afro-American Studies and have read much of the historiography about the Jim Crow era. As a result, my understanding of the time period has become increasingly more detailed and complicated. However, despite all the other books I have read and the primary research I have done, *Black Boy* remains at the core of my emotional understanding of what it was like to grow up in the segregated South, how Jim Crow looked, how it felt. When I think about southern poverty, I conjure up an image of young Richard attempting to sell his beloved pet poodle, Betsy, for a dollar to buy some food. In many ways that image captures the distilled essence of Jim Crow. That single, powerful scene from Wright's autobiography eloquently and poignantly summarizes a mountain of quantitative data about black, southern poverty. I return to *Black Boy* again and again as I try to imagine what that historical moment felt like.

However, my personal, subjective understanding of Jim Crow and my private empathetic connection with Wright have sometimes been difficult to reconcile with the dictates of my scholarly preparation. My historical training taught me that scholars who engage in the study of a past moment must do so "objectively." Because I came of age intellectually during the skeptical era of the twentieth century, I never labored under the nineteenth-century impression that historians were detached scientists who accurately recorded a version of the past that bore no imprint of themselves or the world in which they lived. My understanding of scholarly objectivity comes closest to Michael Stanford's definition. Stanford describes "objectivity as a 'regulative ideal,'" arguing that the idea of objectivity must "guide us as nearly as possible to an impossible goal."[2] We must try to remove our personal biases from our scholarly work at the same time we realize that we can never completely extricate ourselves from our own worldview.

It is difficult—if not impossible—to meld the idea of a somewhat objective understanding of a past world with the purely subjective account of that world as presented in a memoir. After all, the dictates of historical objectivity also tell us that it is possible to tell a history that is true for everyone. However, autobiography recounts the story of only one life. With these concerns in mind, renowned historian A. J. P. Taylor once memorably proclaimed his skepticism about the truth value of first-person accounts of historical events, which he referred to as "old men drooling about their youth."[3] *Had I somehow been misled by my strong identification with Wright?*

I have struggled to reconcile the principles of historical inquiry that demand objectivity with my own subjective, imaginative understanding of Jim Crow. After all, my introduction to the history of the era came in the form of an unabashedly subjective, first-person account of life during segregation. To some extent, this book is an attempt to frame, to analyze, to explain the kind of influence *Black Boy* had on my historical understanding. However, my examination of memoirs as historical source material has implications that reach far beyond *Black Boy*, beyond my own encounter with autobiographical writing, and beyond the Jim Crow era.

It is my contention that the subjective, firsthand character of autobiographies actually enhances their value as a historical source. As John Inscoe argues, "Autobiographers can bring the past alive in ways that more objective scholarly historians rarely do, and as such, engage us in ways that certainly no history textbook or monograph can."[4] In fact, life writing has the potential to enrich our historical understanding in ways that cannot be replicated in any other single source material. In order to understand the kind of impact that autobiography can have on us, we must complicate our thinking about the nature of historical understanding. Furthermore, we also must pay careful attention to the issue of literary style. I found Wright's work so affecting not only because of *what* he said but also because of *how* he said it.

The major claim of this book, broadly stated, is that there are certain aspects of historical reality that can best be captured by artfully wrought literary memoirs. Skillful autobiographers are uniquely equipped to describe the entire universe as it appeared from an acknowledged perspective. Skillfully executed life writing has the ability to portray the complicated interplay between the thoughts and emotions of a historical actor. Furthermore, autobiographers intermingle historical data about what actually happened with reflections on what the author wishes had happened or imagines had happened. A full-fledged understanding of a particular historical moment must capture the complexities of the cognitive and the affective, the factual and the imaginary, perceptions and misperceptions. These elements are constitutive of a complex historical reality, which exists *from* the perspectives of the people who inhabited a past social world. The thought and feelings of historical agents are not responses to a preexisting social reality. Rather, they *are* reality. If we are to come to a deep understanding of a historical moment, we must endeavor to understand the individual experiences that constituted it. No other single source of historical evidence can capture these intricacies as effectively as a literary memoir.

Autobiography is a peculiar genre: it purports to be both literature and history but is not entirely one or the other. Memoirs claim to convey facts and are rooted in real historical events, thus making them appear to be logical resources for the writing of history. However—and this is particularly true in the case of memoirs written by skilled creative writers—autobiographies utilize literary devices and aesthetic power to render emotional truths that cannot be conveyed through a mere recitation of facts.

Despite these obvious parallels with history and literature, it is inadequate to describe the memoir using a strict literature/history dichotomy. Autobiographers assume the role of literary artist in the process of actually writing their book, of historian when claiming to accurately describe past events, and of something else altogether when commenting on events as they unfold or when reflecting broadly on the social structure of their community. Autobiographers frequently assume the role of lay sociologist and cultural critic, and they always function as a cultural anthropologist of sorts—for what are autobiographers if not participant-observers living their life with a critical eye and then reporting their findings later?

The autobiography is a distinct thing in and of itself. It is not merely a peculiar kind of novel or a first-person history. Nonetheless, theorists most frequently position autobiography between the poles of history and literature, describing it, as James Olney did, as something of a "stepchild" of each discipline.[5] Herbert Leibowitz also utilizes a familial analogy to characterize the genre, describing it as a "foster child" of literature, implying that it has no direct biological descent but has instead been adopted by the field.[6] In a sense, Leibowitz's characterization may be more accurate if we conceptualize autobiography as a unique genre rather than a mysterious hybrid.

Until the nineteenth century, autobiographies (frequently referred to as "memoirs") were generally conceived of as historical writings.[7] However, this view was to change with the professionalization of the field of history and the accompanying adoption of the Rankean paradigm of history as an objective science. Under this paradigm, advocated by the German historian Leopold von Ranke (1795–1886), historians were prompted to understand the past on its own terms via a rigorous, scientific examination of primary documents. According to Jeremy Popkin, during this era "memoirs were reduced to the status of mere sources."[8] Memoirs, being anything but objective, no longer qualified as history, which was now the domain of a new class of professional historians. Yet even as the new professional historians were no longer considering memoirs to be history, some literary scholars were originally reluctant to adopt autobiography wholeheartedly as literature because of its claim of reference to real events. Some literary critics thought that the relationship with real events would place strictures on the imaginative aspects of the writing; therefore autobiography could not be as finely crafted as fiction. Besides, the genre had been tainted by its long association with history (which now proclaimed itself a "science"), and literature was, of course, considered *art*. This stalemate of sorts more or less held until the field of autobiographical criticism exploded in the mid-twentieth century.

Despite this unresolved tension about the disciplinary proprietorship of life writing, autobiography has been widely used as a form of evidence in both history and literature. However, for a long time scholars utilized life writing without the benefit of a coherent theoretical framework that took into account its generic peculiarities. A newfound interest in the genre of autobiography began in the 1950s with the publication of Georges Gusdorf's seminal essay "Conditions and Limits of Autobiography."[9] In the United States, interest in autobiography studies exploded in the 1970s and has scarcely abated since. In 1977, Robert F. Sayre christened the autobiography as the "proper study" for students of American studies, claiming that "autobiographies in all their bewildering number and variety offer the student of American Studies a broader and more direct contact with American experience than any other kind of writing."[10]

Nothing summarizes the current en vogue status of autobiographical studies as succinctly as the addition in 2001 of *Autobiography*, by Linda Anderson, to Routledge's New Critical Idiom series. This series is designed to provide students with an entrée into the kind of jargon-laden critical discussions that are generally inaccessible to the novice. With this recent publication, the critical literature about autobiography is implicitly linked with theoretical discussions as wide ranging as postcolonialism, intertextuality, historicism, and romanticism (topics that also claim titles in the series). As we enter the twenty-first century, autobiography is no longer, as it once was, the domain of a handful of specialists but rather one of the cornerstones of literary study. The 2001 publication of the exhaustive two-volume *Encyclopedia of Life Writing*, edited by Margaretta Jolly, further illustrates that autobiographical study has intellectually come of age and has garnered enough interest and critical literature to warrant encyclopedic summaries. Indeed, to keep abreast of contemporary literary theory, one must become acquainted with autobiography studies.

This outpouring of scholarly interest in the autobiography has been led by literary critics and has been concerned with a wide variety of interpretive and theoretical issues. The overwhelming area of interest among scholars of autobiography studies is the issue of how autobiographers represent (or create) individual selves. With the notable exception of Paul John Eakin, most autobiographical critics have not asked whether autobiographies accurately represent an extratextual reality. In some instances this lack of emphasis on the historical nature of the autobiography is rooted in skepticism about the reliability of historical knowledge or in a reluctance to privilege the idea of historical truth. With some consternation, Eakin has noted a shift in autobiography studies from "a documentary view of autobiography as a record of referential fact to a performative view of autobiography centered on the act of composition."[11]

Historians have long used autobiographies as historical sources, mining them for insights into an extratextual past. Although historians have continuously turned to the memoir as a source that can help flesh out the emotional texture of a time period, they have not applied the same kind of theoretical acumen to analyzing the memoir as that applied by their colleagues working in other disciplines. Most historians have analyzed the memoir as if it were any other primary source. On a fundamental level, there is nothing interpretively wrong with this approach. The same basic rules apply to the memoir as to any other source material. We must ascertain the author's identity, his or her audience, motives, and so on. We must also read autobiographies in conjunction with other historical evidence. However, in order to capitalize on the memoir's full revelatory potential, we must adopt a more self-conscious approach to the use of the memoir as a historical source. We must combine the literary critic's tendency to analyze memoirs in their entirety and to identify general principles that can be used in the analysis of autobiographies with the historian's belief that the primary referent of the memoir is an extratextual past reality.

Before I launch a full-blown theoretical discussion about the uses of the memoir as a historical tool, a few words about the problem of defining the genre are in order. Autobiographical theorists have written at length about the problem of autobiographical classification.[12] The issue becomes complicated by the existence of many novels written to appear as autobiographies as well as autobiographies constructed to read as novels. According to Philippe Lejeune's well-known definition, autobiography is a "retrospective prose narrative written by a real person concerning his own existence. . . . In order for there to be autobiography . . . the *author, narrator*, and *protagonist* must be identical."[13] Most critics, at least those who believe in the possibility of constructing an airtight generic classification in the first place, agree in general with Lejeune's definition. However, the problem of establishing whether the author is a "real person" cannot be solved on formalistic grounds alone.

A comparison between the name on the spine of the book and the name of the protagonist inside cannot establish that the name refers to a real, historical person. My definition of autobiography relies on extratextual verification of the existence of the autobiographer. In this regard I stray from the orthodoxies of some literary critics who want to view texts as ontologically independent from authors. Embracing what some would regard as an "intentional fallacy," I find that the intentions of the autobiographer/historical agent are vitally important both interpretively and generically.[14] When deciding which works should be analyzed as autobiographical, we must look for the author's stated intentions to write autobiography.

Paisley Livingston's understanding of intentionalism is particularly useful in this regard. He reunites an author's intentions with a work's meaning without simplistically equating the two within his framework of "moderate intentionalism." He defines moderate intentionalism as "the thesis that the *actual* maker(s)' attitudes and doings are responsible for some of the work's content, and as such are a legitimate target of interpretive claims. . . . [K]nowledge of some, but not all intentions is necessary to some, but not all valuable interpretive insights."[15] Intentionalism of this type does not rule out the possibility of alternate or multiple readings of a text. Nor does it claim that an author's intentions are necessarily realized in the finished product.

Furthermore, Jerrold Levinson makes a valuable distinction between *categorical* intentions and *semantic* intentions. Categorical intentions refer to a maker's decision to make a particular kind of work. This kind of intention "govern[s] not what a work is to mean but how it is to be conceived, approached, classified."[16] Drawing on Levinson's framework, we can argue that the author's intention to create autobiography secures its generic status as autobiography but that the author's intentions alone cannot be conflated with the work's total meaning. After all, it would be a violation of the principles of analysis commonly embraced by both literary critics and historians if we were to conflate the author's intentions with a work's total meaning. We must read any text with a great deal of skepticism.

In addition to looking at the author's intention to write autobiography, we must look to the historical record for confirmation when we decide whether a work is autobiographical. It is conceivable that authors could lie about their intentions to tell their life story and then pass off fiction as autobiographical truth. Therefore we cannot rely on intentions alone. A text cannot be analyzed as autobiographical if the majority of the people, places, and events discussed in the text cannot be externally verified. Although some exaggerating, misremembering, and even lying are invariably part of the autobiographical undertaking, we must make sure that most of the content of the text rings historically true. Readers turn to autobiography with a certain expectation for truth in mind. As Popkin reminds us, life writing is distinct from fiction in part because novelists cannot lie whereas autobiographers can.[17] The historical study of memoirs must be as engaged with the context in which the autobiography is written as it is with the text itself.

The first two chapters of this book examine some of the theoretical issues involved when analyzing autobiography as a historical resource. Chapter 1 tackles the issue of historical objectivity, the topic that initially troubled me as I tried to make sense of the impact that *Black Boy* had on my own historical understanding. I argue that historical reality is inherently perspectival. We cannot understand any social reality outside the perspectives of the people who created and inhabited that social world. In our historical inquiry we must embrace subjectivity and endeavor to understand the way different individuals conceptualized (and created) their social world. In particular, we must attempt to connect empathetically with past historical agents and cultivate an emotional understanding of different historical eras. Chapter

2 expands on my thinking about the potential that life writing has to impact our historical understanding. I argue that skillfully written memoirs, which were designed to be not only historical documents but also works of art, are uniquely able to capture the felt experience of living in history. Gifted creative writers use their literary skills to convey multidimensional and sometimes contradictory layers of their past experiences, which simply cannot be captured by straightforward, literal prose.

The second half of the book is an application of the methodology articulated in the first two chapters. In chapters 3 and 4, I shift my discussion away from general questions about how autobiography can best be used as a historical resource and begin to look closely at several autobiographies written about life in the southern United States during the era of segregation. The Jim Crow era, as it has been dubbed, began at the end of Reconstruction, when southern whites used a variety of techniques—ranging from outright intimidation to literacy tests—to deprive the newly freed slaves of the franchise promised to them by the Fifteenth Amendment. Furthermore, during the 1890s southern states began passing segregation laws, which legitimized the growing custom of providing separate public facilities for whites and for blacks. This grim period of U.S. history endured until civil rights legislation of the mid-1960s outlawed segregation and restored the franchise to black southerners.

The Jim Crow era was characterized by almost unparalleled racial violence and intimidation. Once the region's black people could no longer be counted as personal property, their lives became cheap to many. This period was the era of lynching, which was used as a particularly gruesome means of intimidation and social control. During this time, the entire southern social order was designed to limit the educational and economic prospects of African Americans and to force them into remaining a cheap, tractable supply of labor for white households and white agricultural enterprise.

Strangely, this time period received its nickname "Jim Crow" from a minstrel character invented by the white performer Thomas D. "Daddy" Rice.[18] Rice made his debut as the character "Jim Crow" in an 1828 performance. He wore tattered clothing, darkened his face with burned cork, and painted on exaggerated red lips. He then began to dance and sing a song that he claimed to have learned from an elderly black man. The chorus went:

Wheel about, turn about,
Do jus so,
An' ebery time I wheel about
I jump Jim Crow.

Minstrel acts like Rice's were one of the most popular forms of entertainment in the nineteenth century and attracted large and enthusiastic crowds who enjoyed seeing theatrical portrayals of stereotypical "happy darkies." The adoption of the term "Jim Crow" to identify the era of southern segregation points to the debased notions of blackness and of black people common during the era. However, this unlikely moniker also captures something of the complexity of the historical experience of the individuals who inhabited that social world, something of the irony of that time period. Rice's portrayal of this African American character demonstrates his lack of understanding of or empathy for the richness and tragedy of the black, southern experience. The Jim Crow character represented the happy, carefree, subservient black man, which the white South wanted to see. Lurking behind that happy one-dimensional facade were a wide variety of layered, nuanced black Jim Crow experiences, which Rice's paying customers could not or would not acknowledge.

In order to gain insights into black Jim Crow experiences, I expand on my early fascination with Wright and investigate how two other African American writers memorialized the time period as well. In chapter 3, I examine *Black Boy*; *Dust Tracks on a Road*, written by Zora Neale Hurston, a Wright contemporary; and *Colored People*, written by Harvard academician Henry Louis Gates Jr. A close reading of each of these texts reveals that there was no singular "black" Jim Crow experience. Wright, Hurston, and Gates each assign different degrees of emphasis to the impact of white oppression on their felt Jim Crow experiences. Their descriptions of the black community also differ in a number of respects.

Although it makes sense both interpretively and ethically to place the black, southern experience at the heart of our understanding of the time period, we cannot endeavor to truly understand Jim Crow without investigating white characterizations of the era as well. In chapter 4, I examine the Jim Crow memories of several white southerners: Willie Morris, author of *North Toward Home*; Lillian Smith, author of *Killers of the Dream*;

and William Alexander Percy, author of *Lanterns on the Levee*. All three memoirists capture different aspects of what it was like to be socialized as a white racist. Morris and Smith do so from the perspective of white liberals who have repudiated their racist upbringings, while Percy defends southern race relations. An examination of these memoirs brings a greater degree of complexity to our Jim Crow understanding, as we see that southern segregation had a profound psychological impact on members of the upper tier of the caste system as well as on the region's African American inhabitants. The concluding chapter reconsiders all six memoirs in comparison with one another and shows how they collectively provide sensitive readers with insights into multiple felt experiences of Jim Crow.

Peter N. Stearns and Jan Lewis, scholars working in the field of the history of emotions, argue that one part of the historian's task may be "an attempt to recover that living presence, to capture the way that history felt."[19] Felt experience of any time period is as diverse as the number of historical subjects; it is multiple and it is subjective. If we are to endeavor to apprehend the historical reality of life in the South during the first decades of the twentieth century, then we must embrace Wright, Hurston, Gates, Morris, Smith, and Percy. Historical understanding does not consist of taking sides or of christening certain points of view as representative. All viewpoints, all life experiences, collectively constitute the historical reality of the time period. Nowhere are the worldviews of different individuals as neatly captured as in the well-written, literary memoir.

CHAPTER ONE

Subjectivity and the Felt Experience of History

LIFE WRITING is unabashedly subjective. Sometimes autobiographers claim to speak for members of their entire race or social class; however, within the group the writer claims to represent, there are always members who resent the imposition, who claim that the autobiographer in question "does not speak for me." Of course, because past evidence is always fragmentary, the historian must often ask the historical subjects about whom she or he has the most information to stand in for those whose direct imprint she or he cannot find in the historical record. In other words, historians must extrapolate from what evidence they have if they are ever to compose an overview of a particular era. No doubt certain generalizations can be made about similarities in the lived experiences of contemporaries who had a great deal in common, but when we look closely at two different life experiences, at two different autobiographical accounts, we often see that people from the same social milieu perceived and experienced the same moments in quite different ways.

Individual experiences almost always complicate broad historical generalizations. Therefore, there is a certain amount of tension between historical monographs, which claim to describe a particular time period objectively, and autobiographies, which can only meaningfully claim to document the peculiarities of one life. In order to explore the conflict we sense between these quite different attempts to chronicle the past, we must look at the issues of objectivity and subjectivity in historical interpretation.

A quest for scholarly objectivity lies at the heart of traditional conceptions of the discipline of history. However, historians and other scholars have become increasingly skeptical about the possibility or, in some instances, the desirability of such a perspective. Those who still believe that objectivity is achievable have sometimes proved to be suspicious about the value of the memoir, which is unapologetically subjective, as a historical resource. A. J. P. Taylor views life writing this way, claiming that "written memoirs are a form of oral history set down to mislead historians" and are "useless except for atmosphere."[1] Jeremy D. Popkin, one of the few historians to explore the similarities between autobiography and history, explains the misgivings of some historians this way: "Autobiography may sometimes seem like history, but . . . it [is] impossible to maintain the pretense that an autobiography can achieve scholarly objectivity. Historians have long recognized this fact when using other people's autobiographies as historical resources. Standard manuals for students caution them against reliance on these 'least convincing of all personal records.' "[2]

These misgivings aside, memoirs have long been used selectively as historical resources as historians have mined them for anecdotes or for quotations to illustrate a historical point. However, this ad hoc approach to the usage of memoirs glosses over moments when a memoirist might offer contradictory observations or distort or challenge the reigning historiographical interpretation. Memoirists are not obligated to stifle or reconcile contradictions in the same way that the historian must. Because of the diversity of perspectives they capture, memoirs are unwieldy and complicated source material that many historians use only in small doses, choosing for both methodological and interpretive reasons not to analyze memoirs in their entirety.

Those historians who have expressed skepticism about the truth value of oral histories or memoirs as historical resources often do so in the name of "historical objectivity." The birth of modern history as a professionalized field of inquiry in the nineteenth century is founded on the belief that it is the historian's duty, according to Leopold von Ranke, to tell it how it actually happened. Put differently, in 1898 Lord Acton admonished contributors to *Cambridge Modern History* to "understand that . . . our Waterloo must be one that satisfies French and English, Germans and Dutch alike."[3] Acton's remarks express the belief that a professional historian should let the facts speak for themselves and that a proper assemblage of historical facts must produce an interpretation that corresponds to a reality existing outside that interpretation. According to this extreme vision of historical objectivity, all competent historians looking at the same body of historical data should come to the same conclusions. However, it quickly becomes clear (the best of intentions aside) that this is frequently not the case, and the notion of "objectivity" is then thrown into crisis.

Thomas Nagel convincingly argues that there are many things that simply cannot be understood from an objective standpoint. He says, "A great deal is essentially connected to a particular point of view or a type of point of view, and the attempt to give a complete account of the world in objective terms detached from these perspectives brings us into error."[4] Furthermore, Michael Stanford argues, "Fully to understand their doings and their predicaments it is necessary to enter, as far as possible, into their perceptions, their reactions, their calculations, their emotions."[5] The subjectivity of historical agents is not something we should try to guard against but something we should embrace as a vehicle for a richer understanding of the past.

What Taylor derides as "atmosphere" is actually itself part of the historical reality the historian is trying to uncover. The way individual narrators perceived, experienced, and described their individual lives is itself history, which by its very nature is subjective. Because historical perspectives are as numerous as historical agents, understanding an event from every possible perspective is impossible. Unfortunately there are not enough memoirs to document every historical event or to represent each geographical location in each historical era. Even where memoirs do exist, they do not always represent a wide cross section of society. However, when we do have access to a wide spectrum of memoirs, our historical understanding is richer, and we are put in touch with the experiential aspects of living in history.

The view of historical reality I maintain is multifaceted; it is a view in which truth is in many cases perspectival. Understandably this concept threatens the idea that one can write monographs that even approach being comprehensive or definitive. Popkin has studied the attempts of many historians to write their own autobiographies and claims that this enterprise is complicated because "they are often acutely conscious that their own stories complicate or contradict the generalizations they and their colleagues have painstakingly elaborated, the 'grand narratives' in which the discipline has encoded collective experience."[6] When we have access to the recorded experiences of individual historical agents, our historical understanding is certainly richer, but we also become more aware of how necessarily incomplete our understanding of history is and of how many voices from the past remain unheard. To think of history as multiperspectival, with each individual experience at variance with the experiences of others, makes the historians' task of re-creating the past even more daunting.

Historical objectivity is generally understood in two ways. The first way it is defined is as "value-neutral." This version of the doctrine of historical objectivity is focused on the act of writing history itself. Following the guidelines of historical objectivity conceptualized this way, historians should survey the historical evidence and generate historiography that does not bear the imprint of the historians' own personally held viewpoints. That historians are *not* being objective is frequently apparent if their interpretation bears the obvious imprint of their nationalistic identification or ideological persuasion. But objectivity of this kind is a quality that is easier to identify in its absence than its presence.

All historians are, of course, influenced by the times in which they are living, by their ideological perspectives, by the kinds of historical resources they choose to utilize, by the politics of the academy, and by their individual life experiences among other things. A belief in value-neutral historiography rests on the assumption that historians can put aside these personal viewpoints and sketch a detached "objective" portrait of the past. But often historians are unaware of how deeply held their own beliefs are and to what extent they influence their interpretations. For example, a historian's deeply held racism could influence the kind of history he or she writes. Indeed, race has traditionally been a blind spot in American historiography.

In 1935 W. E. B. Du Bois effectively called into question the prevailing Dunning school interpretation of Reconstruction—which depicted the white South as having been victimized by unscrupulous and incompetent northerners and freedpeople—by writing his own study of the time period, empowered with the idea that "Negroes were ordinary human beings."[7] Similarly, Jefferson scholars who were blinded by their own racism refused to believe that the founding father could have had a long-standing sexual relationship with his slave Sally Hemings until DNA evidence demonstrated that the third president does indeed have both black and white descendants. Racism has been so interwoven in American culture that historians of Reconstruction writing in the Dunning school tradition and many Jefferson scholars could not see their way around it when interpreting history. There is no reason to believe that we have not been similarly blindsided in many aspects of our current historical understanding.

The idea that historians can ever completely remove their own viewpoints from the writing of history has been discarded by most members of the historical profession. Historians have been set free to question how, where, and why their own perspectives color their interpretation of history. And yet, since historians can never completely escape the confines of their own perspective, such an interrogation is in the end compromised by their ultimate imprisonment inside their own worldview.

The second way in which historical objectivity is defined is in terms of the Rankean conception that it is possible to write a history that corresponds directly with a real past, a history that will then be equally true for each historical agent who participated in that past. The belief that a historiographical account can ever accurately represent the past it purports to illuminate, however, is largely a matter of faith. Just as witnesses observing a historical event are limited by their individual perspectives, historians are also confined by their own point of view; they cannot even hope to know the "whole story" of the moments they have lived, let alone the whole story of a particular historical moment. It is therefore impossible to compare a witness's observation of a historical moment with a historian's version of that moment and conclude with certainty that the historian's version corresponds directly with the real past. In other words, there is no way to "test" a historian's objectivity by comparing his or her interpretation with a real past, since neither the historian nor the historical agents who lived that past are able to access it completely.

Both ideals of historical objectivity (value neutrality and correspondence with historical reality) are now generally, if sometimes grudgingly, viewed as ultimately unattainable. Michael Stanford suggests that "we might do well to admit objectivity as a 'regulative ideal,' so that it may guide us as nearly as possible to an impossible goal."[8] This approach is more or less the tacit compromise most historians have made with the dictates of their field. Objectivity is something historians strive for, all the while knowing that it is impossible to attain.

The conception that there is a historical truth (however difficult to arrive at) that is actually true for all historical agents is ultimately a problematic one. According to Peter Novick, the concept of objectivity asserts that "truth is one, not perspectival."[9] The implications of this claim have an obvious impact on memoir studies. The genre of the memoir is founded on the idea that memoirs make truth claims about the past. However, these claims are often very different from memoir to memoir. Generally a skeletal body of agreed-on facts emerges when reading a body of memoirs that recount the same historical moment, but the way these facts are interpreted and experienced by individual memoirists often differs wildly. Different memoirists have witnessed different events and interacted with different people and thus report specific experiences unduplicated in other accounts. Although this fact in itself is not conceptually problematic, it does make the verification of individual accounts by means of corroborating witnesses (a cardinal rule among most historians) impossible to achieve in some instances. However, significantly, sometimes memoirists have witnessed the same event but perceived it much differently than have other memoirists. How, then, is the historian to decide which version is true? Is it possible that these varying accounts are simultaneously contradictory and true?

Because there are no easy answers to these questions, modern historians as a whole are much more skeptical about the possibility of achieving historical objectivity than were their Rankean predecessors. That being said, historians have also proved quite reluctant to dispense entirely with the concept of objectivity. Part of this reluctance stems from fears of encroachment by literary studies and a desire to keep history separate. If historians were to dispense altogether with the belief in their ability to make objective truth claims, many fear that history would be conflated with the study of fiction and historians would essentially become no different than literary critics. Sir Geoffrey Elton has voiced extreme hostility toward the possibility of utilizing both literature and the techniques of literary criticism in the study of history by opining somewhat hysterically, "In battling against people who would subject historical studies to the dictates of literary critics, we historians are, in a way, fighting for our lives. Certainly, we are fighting for the lives of innocent young people beset by devilish tempters who claim to offer higher forms of thought and deeper truths and insights—the intellectual equivalent of crack."[10] Elton's concern is shared by, among others, Keith Windschuttle, who in 1996 published a book-length "defense" of history none too subtly entitled *The Killing of History: How Literary Critics and Social Theorists Are Murdering Our Past.*[11]

So what is it that these figurative crack dealers are pushing, which if ingested is capable of "killing" the discipline of history? According to Windschuttle, literary critics and social theorists can be indicted on three counts. He finds critics and theorists, poststructuralists in particular, guilty of "undermin[ing] the methodology of historical research," "destroy[ing] the distinction between history and fiction," and erroneously believing "that it is impossible to access the past [and furthermore] that we have no proper grounds for believing that a past independent of ourselves ever took place."[12] Although each of his accusations would make an interesting starting point for a discussion of how the methodology and assumptions of theorists and historians sometimes differ, let us concentrate on his third allegation. The debate over whether a past independent of our textual representations of that past actually exists is at the heart of the tension between literary and historical perspectives.

It is an obvious simplification to speak of the "literary perspective" and the "historical perspective" as if such unified and coherent viewpoints actually exist. Indeed, there are as many variations and combinations of beliefs as there are scholars. In referring to the tension between literary and historical perspectives, I am talking specifically about how some poststructuralist theories, which have been embraced to some degree by many (but not all) literary theorists, have called into question an underlying belief in a knowable past, which is held by most (but not all) historians. Because the study of the memoir as historical source material is embedded in a belief in a real and (to some extent) knowable past, it is necessary to examine this conflict further.

Paul John Eakin has observed that scholars working in the field of autobiography studies are much more likely to focus on the act of writing autobiography than on any reality external to the text, noting that "the reality of the past seems quite simply to vaporize."[13] In some cases autobiographical critics have reduced the study of autobiography to a study of texts alone without reference to any context, authorial or historical. Roland Barthes poses the viewpoint held by many theorists with a rhetorical question embedded in his own attempt at autobiography, "Do I not know that, *in the field of the subject, there is no referent?*"[14]

Barthes is articulating a widespread point of view held in variations and degrees by theorists such as Derrida and Foucault and their adherents who claim that language is a kind of prison or a closed system that refers endlessly only to itself rather than to a reality that exists outside language. Michel Foucault's relationship to historians and to the historical profession was an ambivalent one. His own writings straddle the disciplines of philosophy and history, but he remained somewhat suspicious of historians and their quest for historical knowledge, remarking in 1982, "I am not a professional historian; nobody is perfect."[15] One of Foucault's greatest criticisms of professional historiography is of what he saw as its arrogant quest for perfection, the perfection of historical truth. He characterized historians as demagogues, arguing, "As the demagogue is obliged to invoke truth, laws of essences, and eternal necessity, the historian must invoke objectivity, the accuracy of facts, and the permanence of the past."[16] Foucault particularly objected to the historical search for "origins," the idea that a historian can trace a historical event, idea, or institution "back to a sort of founding era or moment when their essential meaning was first revealed" and up into the present in a linear, historical progression.[17] Foucault rejects the idea of origins, just as he rejects the idea of essence or truth. According to Michael Confino, Foucault "rejects history *because* it assumes 'reality, identity, truth.' By the same token, historical discourse and historical writing melt entirely and disappear (or do not exist at all except in figments of the imagination and representational fallacies), since historical discourse without referent reality is nothing but fiction."[18]

The effect of this theory on the enterprise of professional historiography is potentially devastating. As Confino further argues, theory of this kind "posits, in the last analysis, that the writing of history is impossible; that language is indeterminate and, therefore, that historical events in the past cannot be narrated or analyzed; or, alternatively, that they can be narrated and analyzed in an infinite number of ways, none of which is more (or less) truthful than the others."[19] Many literary theorists have accepted the conflation of context and text, either explicitly or implicitly by failing to actively engage what Paul John Eakin declares is the "commonplace assumption for students of autobiography . . . that the past is a fiction."[20] Eakin remains one of the few literary critics to actively fight the easy acceptance of the belief that autobiographies (along with other texts) refer only to themselves and that the bridge between signifiers and real-world signifieds cannot be traversed. He bluntly argues, "In the age of poststructuralism we have been too ready to assume that the very idea of a referential aesthetic is untenable, but autobiography is nothing if not a referential act."[21]

Historians as a whole have been far more reluctant than their colleagues in literature departments to dispose of the idea that autobiographies and other historical source material refer to a real past that exists independently, that is, outside historical documents. Historians are often criticized for what many poststructural theorists and historical constructivists see as naive realism. However, most critiques of this kind are based on a version of extreme realism maintained by few, if any, practicing historians. According to P. H. Nowell-Smith, this mythical extreme historical realist is "one who holds that the touchstone of historical truth must be direct observation of or an acquaintance with the object concerned."[22] Since the past is gone and irretrievable and direct observation is impossible, this thesis of extreme realism quickly becomes untenable. Furthermore, the thoughts and emotions of historical agents are, as we shall see, part of the historical reality that the historian is trying to uncover, and neither would be accessible by means of direct observation were such observation possible in the first place.

So, if the direct observation required by extreme realism is impossible when the past is the object of inquiry, what kind of realism do historians maintain that does not rely on such observation? Chris Lorenz argues that "contrary to widespread postmodern fashion—historians always claim knowledge of a real past; and as all claims of knowledge embody truth claims the justification of truth claims must remain equally central to history."[23] Lorenz attempts to navigate what he regards as the "swamps of positivism and the quicksands of postmodernism" by adapting Hilary Putnam's concept of "internalism" or what Lorenz labels "internal realism."[24] According to Putnam, internalism "hold[s] that *what objects does the world consist of?* is a question that only makes sense to ask *within* a theory of description. . . . [Furthermore,] there is more than one 'true' theory or description of the world."[25] Lorenz acknowledges the fact "that our knowledge of reality is mediated through language," but he does not draw the conclusion that language constitutes reality.[26] Although our only access to the past comes through historians' descriptions of the past, those descriptions should not be mistaken for the past itself, which Lorenz insists exists independently, outside our knowledge thereof. Lorenz allows for the possibility of multiple true historical claims, arguing that each is true within its own "specific frame of description."[27] Because we cannot compare historians' claims to the actual past, we cannot ultimately decide on a correct interpretation but rather must evaluate each historical interpretation for its coherence within its own framework. As Putnam observes, there is no "God's eye" point of view to serve as a final arbitrator of what is true. Instead, we are left with "various points of view of actual persons reflecting various interests and purposes that their descriptions and theories subserve."[28] "Internal realism" provides a useful framework for memoir studies because it maintains a belief in a real past that exists external to the textual retelling of the past even while it acknowledges that historical truth often looks different depending on where one is standing—both literally and figuratively. The idea that historical truth is perspectival is particularly pertinent to the study of historical memoirs.

Historians Joyce Appleby, Lynn Hunt, and Margaret Jacob have called for a "practical realism" that is "different, more nuanced, less absolutist . . . than that championed by an older . . . naïve realism."[29] Realism of this kind recognizes that historiography cannot precisely mirror the past; there is always a gap between reality and our representations of it. Practical realism also acknowledges that history is largely interpretive, that historians invariably construct even as they attempt to reconstruct elements of the past. However, the fact that historians bring their own interpretations to bear on historical documents does not lead Appleby, Hunt, and Jacob to embrace what they consider the nihilism, extreme skepticism, and relativism of poststructuralism. Instead, they steadfastly maintain that "some words and conventions, however socially constructed, reach out into the world and give a reasonably true description of its contents."[30]

Ultimately the belief that historians are able even somewhat accurately to describe a past that is removed from us is largely a matter of faith. As Robert Anchor observes, "This belief [in realism] can no more be proved or disproved than its opposite: that there is nothing beyond language, that 'reality' is a world of words without end."[31] However, even if a belief in a real past and our potential to uncover knowledge about that past is largely a matter of faith, it is a matter of faith that is crucial both to history and to memoir studies.

The genre of autobiography rests on the concept of reference. Identity between the author of the autobiography and the protagonist in the autobiography is what makes a work autobiographical. Without authorial context there can be no autobiography. Furthermore, autobiographers are historical agents who are simultaneously documenting history as they perceived it and attempting to shape the way their readers remember that history. Without belief in a past external to the text, autobiographical narrators are stripped of agency, of their potential both to affect the way the past is remembered and to use their autobiographical accounts as political tools either to support the status quo or to agitate for change. Without accepting the existence of a knowable social reality, both past and present, that autobiographers are both reacting to and attempting to create, the auto-biographical project becomes meaningless. As Robert Anchor succinctly remarks, we simply "cannot live in a wholly meaningless world."[32] A foundational belief in a practical realism, such as that held by most practicing historians, restores meaning by restoring context, which is crucial to my conception of memoir studies aesthetically, generically, and politically.

The historical study of memoirs is embedded in a belief that the memoir refers to a real (and to some extent knowable) past and is sympathetic to the practicing historian's tendency to emphasize the particular and historically situated over the theoretical and general. However, because memoirs are works of literature as well as history, they often transcend the particular and become universally relevant. The historical study of memoirs combines history and theory. Memoirs offer valuable insights into specific historical moments, but they might also shed light on general truths that go beyond one isolated era.

It is simply not possible to write, to understand, or to experience history from an "objective" standpoint. Rather, history is experienced, recorded, and understood subjectively. The historical study of memoirs emphasizes the subjective nature of history, with specific concentration on the power that each memoirist was able to exercise in both shaping and reporting on her or his own life. Memoirs are uniquely able to give us insights into the past because they represent the viewpoints of individual historical actors and are, by their very nature, subjective.

Wilhelm Dilthey argued that "the course of an individual life in the environment in which it is affected and which it affects" is "the germinal cell of history."[33] If we accept this conception of history, it follows, as Dilthey further claimed, that "autobiography is the highest and most instructive form in which the understanding of life confronts us."[34] Although biographies and historiographical writing may describe the events of an individual's life, they are ill equipped to describe how a historical subject felt or how a historical subject perceived his or her own life. In biography or history, such topics are left to conjecture or are the outgrowth of analyses of the writings or recorded conversations of the biographical subject. However, the autobiography presents a cohesive and carefully constructed account of what living through a particular historical moment looked like and felt like from the perspective of the autobiographer.

R. G. Collingwood, an influential philosopher of history, describes historical reality in terms of individual historical actors. He begins his description of historical reality by contrasting the study of history with the study of the natural world. According to Collingwood, historical reality is fundamentally unlike natural reality and thus cannot be studied using the same methodology.[35] In order to describe the differences between natural processes and historical ones, he describes "the inside and outside" of events. Natural events have only an outside component. They are "mere events."[36] The observable facts that leaves change color in the autumn or that water freezes or boils at certain temperatures are phenomena that occur in accordance with physical laws that are not the product of thought. In contrast, human beings are capable of thought, and to understand the social world in either the past or the present, we must take into account that humans, unlike objects in the natural world, have the capability for reason. Unlike natural events, historical events have both an inside and an outside.

The outside of a historical event consists of the placement and movement of bodies in a given historical moment. Even if time travel were possible and we were able to watch a historical moment unfold, we would be unable to comprehend the event through observation alone. Collingwood's classic example of this truth is the assassination of Caesar. A mere physical description of Caesar's lifeless body and the location of the bodies of the individuals responsible for his death would describe only part of the historical reality of the event. In order to understand this or any other historical event, we must look at the inside of the event, which consists of the thought of the historical agents.

According to Collingwood, "all history is the history of thought."[37] True historical understanding is the understanding of the inside of a historical event and comes as a result of reenacting past thought. The historian must actively and critically attempt to rethink the thoughts of a historical agent in order to understand the agent's motivations and justifications for acting in a certain way. Because historians are human beings who are studying other human beings, the historian is able to identify closely with the subjects of historical inquiry. Historians thus stand in direct contrast to natural scientists, who cannot have the same kind of affinity for the objects they study. Because we cannot directly interact with historical subjects who are no longer living, we must relate to them imaginatively by reenacting their thoughts—or, to put it more colloquially, by putting ourselves in their shoes. As Michael Stanford argues, "We can understand people—inwardly so to speak—largely because we ourselves are human."[38] Dilthey argues that historical understanding consists largely of "the rediscovery of the I in the Thou."[39] In other words, in order to apprehend past reality, historians must draw on similarities between themselves and the historical subject. However, these human similarities transcend the shared capability for rational thought, which Collingwood emphasized.

Collingwood emphasized rationality, arguing that the historian can only hope to rethink rational thought and thus cannot comprehend either the emotions or the irrational thought of a historical agent. Thus, in his formulation, true historical knowledge is possible only when historical actors behaved in a rational manner and were motivated by conscious thought processes—which can be rethought—rather than by unconscious motivations, by passions. Collingwood's understanding of the inside of a historical event is limited in its applicability because of his emphasis on rational thought and conscious motivation. Collingwood is not alone in his emphasis on rationality. Peter N. Stearns and Jan Lewis have observed that "professional historians' epistemology, their underlying assumptions about knowledge and the way it is acquired, has often turned into a set of assumptions about the way people behave. . . . Historians have implied that most people in the past have been more or less rational."[40] This epistemological bent has resulted in the devaluing of the emotional aspects of historical experience.

Human behavior—the inside of a historical event—is not only cognitive but also affective. Humans do not always behave in a rational manner and are not always conscious of what motivates their behavior. The autobiography gives us a unique window into the interplay of thoughts and feelings, into how the universe *felt* from one particular point of view. Using the techniques of literary art, a memoirist finds ways to capture the relationship between purpose, affect, and perceptions and places his or her own thoughts and feelings about a historical moment in relation to those of other people in the same social scene.

Archival materials, which are not works of literature, frequently cannot capture this complex reality, particularly when viewed in isolation. Historians using archival materials may indeed hypothesize about the inside of a historical event, but such interpretations are highly speculative. In studying history without the benefit of literary memoirs, historians must project themselves into a situation and imagine how they would have felt, what they would have thought, and thus how they would have reacted. Where memoirs exist, this kind of speculation is not necessary, for the memoirist him- or herself guides us, telling us what to think and how to feel. The well-crafted memoir enables us, in a way that no other single historical resource can, to reexperience the affective and cognitive inside of a historical moment.

In our attempts to re-create the past on the basis of the clues that we are able to access in the present, we err when we distance ourselves emotionally from the subject of our historical inquiry and content ourselves with unraveling the "what happened in the past?" question without tackling the more evasive but equally intriguing question "how did it feel?" By daring to ask the second question, we come closer to the historian's goal of understanding the past on its own terms. We must dispense with the tired myth of history as detached and objective, as a science, and embrace Jacques Barzun and Henry F. Graff's inclusive definition of history as "vicarious experience."[41] "Knowledge of history is," according to Barzun and Graff, "like a second life extended indefinitely . . . backward."[42] The memoir, unlike any other genre of historical writing, is uniquely poised to give its reader the chance to live vicariously and, however briefly, to indeed experience "a second life," which is acted out in the interplay between the written word and the reader's historical imagination.

If we conceptualize history, as Barzun does, as "vicarious experience," we can expand Collingwood's doctrine of reenactment beyond the realm of rational thought and "refeel" what historical actors felt. David Stockley has argued that "empathetic reconstruction" is an important aspect of historical knowing. In order to "refeel," historians should actually draw on their own life experiences and embrace their shared humanity with the object of their inquiry. Because historians have experienced hope, sorrow, anxiety, and the rest of the spectrum of human emotions, it is possible for them to project their own understanding of those emotions onto the historical subject they are studying. Brian Attebery argues that "we can recognize in the products of the past the same kind of sifting, structuring, and evaluating of experience that we undertake in our own lives."[43] Rather than trying to remove their emotions from their work as the doctrine of historical objectivity dictates, students of history should use their own experiences and emotions as tools to help them understand what it felt like to live in the past.

Not only can a historian identify with the cognitive and affective aspects of historical subjects (largely because the historian, too, is capable of thinking and feeling), but the historian is also aware of the way thoughts and emotions intermingle, sometimes contradict each other, and frequently take on a different significance when transferred from the realm of direct experience into that of memory.

In contrast to Rankean calls for historical objectivity, my conception of the historical study of memoirs emphasizes the subjectivity not only of the memoirist but also of the person analyzing the memoir. Readers cannot hope to understand what it felt like to live through a particular historical moment without allowing themselves to empathize with the memoirist. There are times when empathetic understanding is difficult or even impossible to achieve. Students of history may have difficulty projecting aspects of themselves into an understanding of the actions of notorious or violent historical characters. Indeed, it may be too frightening an exercise even to attempt to identify, no matter how imaginary and tenuous the connection, with the thoughts and emotions of historical villains.

However, it also might be easier to empathize with the thoughts and feelings of evildoers than we would like to think, and in the empathetic identification with people whom we have come to identify as depraved, we might discover darker recesses of ourselves. However, attempting to see the world from the perspective of a particular historical actor should not be confused with a justification or wholehearted embrace of his or her thoughts and values. In trying to understand how it felt to be living at a particular time in history and how the world looked from a particular perspective, the historian is not endorsing or adopting another person's worldview. Empathetic reconstruction can be replayed again and again from the perspective of different historical actors. Such identifications are only temporary and are necessarily moderated by the historian's own ethical concerns and present-minded worldview.

Empathetic reconstruction or refeeling is not purely instinctual; nor is it uncritical. My suggestion that we refeel the emotions of historical agents does not include a suggestion that we dispense with the rational elements of historical understanding. David Stockley insists that "empathetic reconstruction may well be an imaginary act, but it is also an analytical one and one that must be prepared for."[44] To truly "live vicariously" another life in the past, even for just a moment, requires immersion in historical material about a given time period. Individual memoirs should not be read in isolation. Various memoirs from the same time period should be read together and compared with one another. They should also be read along with secondary scholarship about the time period in question so that the reader will notice if certain details or descriptions are at variance with the vast majority of writing about the period. Historical empathy is impossible if certain details ring false, and the historian must verify the feasibility of specific autobiographical accounts. However, the historian must also endeavor to be open minded and to resist the tendency to embrace only autobiographical accounts that fit neatly inside the realm of her or his expectations.

This emphasis on empathetic reconstruction of the thoughts and feelings of individual historical agents reminds us that history contains a multiplicity of perspectives. Memoirists, each of whom is a center of consciousness, interact with other centers of consciousness, individuals who perceive the historical reality of their life differently. Historical reality is composed of the sum total of these individuals' varied experiences. Furthermore, historical reality is inherently perspectival.

Robert Paul Wolff demonstrates the perspectival nature of social reality by first comparing the natural world with the social world, specifically examining the concept of time. Natural events happen in isotropic time. No moment of time is any more important than any other moment. In contrast, human time is anisotropic. Human beings experience some moments as more significant than others. We distinguish between the past, the present, and the future, and each has a different significance to us. Human time is "organized by our affective and evaluative orientation toward the content of moments of time."[45] In distinguishing between moments of time and in making some moments more important than others, we are actually creating the structure of time that will govern our society. The same can be said for other social institutions and social roles. They are constructed by human beings and do not exist outside the perceptions of the humans who create and sustain them.

Following the publication of Peter Berger and Thomas Luckmann's classic text *The Social Construction of Reality: A Treatise in the Sociology of Knowledge* (1966), it has become commonplace for scholars working in a variety of fields to acknowledge the assumption that social reality, unlike natural reality, simply does not exist outside human cognition.[46] Finn Collin succinctly summarizes the theory of social construction, writing:

"Social reality is somehow generated by the way we *think* or *talk* about it, by our *consensus* about its nature, by the way we *explain* it to each other, and by the *concepts* we used to grasp it. Social facts are thought to be a product of the very cognition, the very intellectual processes through which they are cognized, explained, and classified. . . . It is the very intellectual activity that is thought to generate facts."[47]

Money is the classic example often used to explain this phenomenon. The pieces of paper and metal coins that different societies use as currency are not valuable in and of themselves. They are valuable only because the society believes they are, because the social world imbues them with a particular significance. Societies collectively decide that these tokens have a particular worth and can be exchanged to buy things. Without that collective, societal understanding we are left only with slips of paper and pieces of metal. Thus money exists only from the perspective of the society that believes in its value.

Wolff expands on these ideas by comparing social reality to fictional narratives, arguing that the fictional world of a novel "*exists* from the point of view of the narrator."[48] Much like fictional worlds, which exist only from the perspective of the narrator, the social world exists only from the perspective of humans. Wolff argues that "the history of a society is a collective narrative."[49] Thus we can infer that historical reality *exists* from the point of view of the multiple narrators. What, then, is the relationship of individuals to the larger social structure? An individual cannot create a social reality; it is a collective undertaking. If an individual cannot create a social role alone, can an individual fight against it, as an individual? The answer, according to Wolff, is yes. "Those who occupy the roles can embrace the evaluative structure of the role, resist it, play off against it, vary it, but they cannot avoid engaging with it in some way, because that structure is part of what the role *is*."[50] Thus, even though social reality is created collectively, it is also experienced individually. To return to the concept of narrative voice, we can say that different individuals sometimes struggle over who should control "the narrative voice of the story of a society."[51]

Social reality (and therefore historical reality, also) is perspectival on both the societal and individual levels. Social reality and human time do not exist without collective recognition of their attributes. However, this fact cannot completely dictate the way individual agents perceive and interpret their own social roles. The memoir is particularly well suited to illuminate the way individual historical agents "play off . . . vary . . . and engage" with the social roles available to them.

These individual experiences and actions, which are driven by both thoughts and emotions, constitute social reality. The conflicting ideas and perceptions of individual historical agents constitute a many-sided picture of a single historical event. Memoirs are historically revealing even when multiple autobiographers remember the same event differently. They are historically revealing even when memoirists lie or misremember. These thoughts and feelings, perceptions and misperceptions are elements of the historical reality that the historian must try to uncover.

When talking about the interpretation of memoirs as a historical resource, questions about verifiability and truth telling arise again and again. These issues are accompanied by concerns over deliberate lying and also with the way memory operates, particularly in terms of misremembering and reremembering. If we conceive of history, as Hayden White does, as a special kind of fiction, "the contents of which are as much invented as found," we need not trouble ourselves probing historical narratives for truth.[52] However, if we believe that historical writing captures, however imperfectly, aspects of a real but vanished past, we must examine historical resources for the accuracy with which they recall and represent the actual past. That being said, discovered falsehoods and misrepresentations can give us insights into the past, too. Distortions in the historical record can ultimately be just as revealing as they are initially misleading.

When historians analyze the testimony of historical witnesses (regardless of the form these testaments take, whether published memoirs, private diaries, or oral history interviews), they must try to ascertain the truthfulness of their informants and also must evaluate the reliability of their informants' memory. Memoir is at the crossroads of memory and history, and it contains elements of both.

Paul Thompson, an expert on the methodology of oral history, a field with obvious similarities to memoir studies, is scornful of historians who are obsessed with the factual "reliability" of oral histories, claiming that such a preoccupation "obscures the really interesting questions." As Thompson eloquently argues, "Reality and myth, 'objective' and 'subjective,' are inextricably mixed in all human perception of the world."[53] The historian should not push aside the misperceptions of historical agents in the name of recovering "what really happened" in a particular historical moment, for these misunderstandings are an indispensable part of a total understanding of any historical moment.

Luise White claims, "For historians, the invented account is at least as good as the accurate one. . . . Because dissembling is perhaps the most pointed telling we have . . . a lie, a cover story, not only camouflages but explains." In analyzing testimony with dubious literal truth value, the historian might learn a great deal about the way an individual perceived him- or herself and his or her times (if the witness's misrepresentation is honest) or about how the individual would like to be remembered (if his or her lies are more calculated). Cover stories, lies, and distorted truths are often crafted deliberately and the discovered intention to deceive makes "certain information so charged that its value and importance is unlike other information."[54] An uncovered lie might function as a red flag, alerting a historian to an area where he or she should dig a little deeper. For example, in an oral history interview, a slave owner might describe himself as a benevolent, paternalistic master, while plantation records demonstrate that his slaves were malnourished and beaten cruelly. Although the slave owner's testimony seems at odds with the documentary evidence, his pretense of paternalism reveals a great deal about his perception of himself and about the ethos of his community of slaveholders.

Timothy Dow Adams claims that "lying in autobiography is not just something that happens inevitably; rather it is a highly strategic decision, especially on the part of literary autobiographers."[55] If the bulk of a text is harmonious with other historical data yet one or two episodes appear to be fabrications, the historian must analyze the cover story both to find what it initially conceals and to see what the deliberate effort to tell a lie might reveal about the memoirist and her or his society.

Any analysis of written memoirs necessarily touches on the ongoing interdisciplinary discussion about "historical memory." History and memory are similar to the extent that both attempt to reconstruct the past, but they do so on very different terms. According to Pierre Nora in his seminal essay "Between Memory and History," "memory and history, far from being synonymous, appear now to be in fundamental opposition."[56] Memory, according to Nora, is in a state of evolution and has life, while history is a lifeless reconstruction of "what is no longer." Furthermore, memory is "affective and magical," while history is "prosaic."[57] Freed from the strictures of scholarly prose, memoirists are indeed able to capture something of the "magic" of lived experience as they relive experience through memories.

Memoirs share elements of both memory and history. They are a record of memories, certainly, but if we are to accept the idea that memory is dynamic rather than static, a memoir does not remain in the domain of memory for long. After it is written down, it becomes fixed, a set interpretation, somewhat akin to historiography. When memoirists write their life story, they are, in a sense, transforming living memories into a fixed history. Nora refers to memoirs, monuments, anniversaries, and archives as the "materialization of memory."[58] The memoir or the archive is no longer living and in the process of change like memory itself; rather, it is immovable, "a secondary memory, a prosthesis memory."[59]

Although the historical study of memoirs is rooted in the belief that historiographical accounts refer to a real past, history is inevitably partially construction as well as reconstruction of what is no longer. History is constructed when a historian filters through existing data about the past and attempts to build a plausible story of past events. Memory, too, biologists agree, is constructed rather than recalled. "Biologists now support the recent subjectivist thrust in psychology that envisions each memory as an active and new construction made from many tiny associations, not a passive process of storing and retrieving full-blown objective representations of past experiences."[60] Chances are that an individual never remembers the same event quite the same way twice. In memoirs, we are unable to see the stages and alterations of memories that the author experimented with before permanently choosing one "materialization of memory." Memoir writing, like history, like memory itself, is partially reconstruction of lived movements but is invariably a construction, too. The historian should be concerned with understanding the process of historical construction as well as with the outcome.

Memory may be rooted not in real life experiences but rather in the imagination. Harry Crews's memoir of growing up in rural Georgia begins with such a false memory. He claims, "My first memory is of a time ten years before I was born, and the memory takes place where I have never been and involves my daddy whom I never knew."[61] Memoirists capture not only individual memories but also communal understandings of the past.

Memories are in flux, and even the most vivid memories may have no bearing in objective reality but could instead be products of the imagination inspired by someone else's experiences. Memoirs themselves, particularly those written with great aesthetic power, may eventually become a part of their readers' memories. Indeed, a historian might assemble a body of false memories and impressions of a past reality he or she never directly experienced. When reading memoirs, it is important, indeed crucial, to be aware of the mutable nature of memory. However, this awareness should not detract from the historical value to be found in even "false memories" because, as Thompson argues, "one part of history, what people imagined happened, and also what they believe *might* have happened—their imagination of an alternative past, and so an alternative present—may be as crucial as what did happen."[62]

When reading a memoir, it is necessary to attempt to decipher the motivations of the author in writing the memoir and in remembering things in a particular way. The construction of memories, and by extension memoirs, does not occur in "isolation," as David Thelan reminds us, but in the "contexts of community, broader politics, and social dynamics."[63] Among other things, memories and thus memoirs are affected by the writer's gender, political outlook, and social status. Memoirists are in fact filtering and manipulating their own memories in an attempt, conscious or otherwise, to alter the historical memories of their readers. Read this way, the study of historical memory—or for our purposes, historical memoirs—can be understood, as David Blight puts it, "as the study of cultural struggle, of contested truths, of moments, events, or even texts in history that thresh out rival versions of the past which are in turn put to battle in the present."[64]

Thus memoirs give us insights not only into "what really happened" in the past but also into the way the past was remembered. Furthermore, because memory is dynamic and because it is possible to have the sensation of remembering events that one never directly experienced, memoirs continue to influence the way the past is remembered every time they are read. Karen Fields emphatically declares that "our scholarly effort to get the 'real' past, not the true past required by a particular present, does not authorize us to disdain as simply mistaken this enormously consequential, creative, and everywhere visible operation of memory."[65]

The way the past is remembered is often at odds with what really happened. It is the job of the historian, or the scholar of the historical study of memoirs, to compare memoirs and other historical documents in order to compose as complete and as verifiable a depiction of a historical moment as possible. However, this is a job that is never finished. It is ongoing. The way the past is remembered is in a continual dialogue with historical consensus about the true nature of the past. When memories, false and otherwise, compete with history, we must question the political motives of both the person who remembers and the person who chronicles.

Memories are frequently subversive and challenge official histories, which often exclude the experiences of marginalized groups (whether marginalized by gender, religious affiliation, race, socioeconomic status, nationality, or other factors). Milan Kundera poetically declares that "the struggle of man against power is the struggle of memory against forgetting."[66] Memory of this kind is emancipatory. It fights against fixed historical interpretations that silence dissenting voices. Memory of this kind is revealed in the oral histories of former slaves who show that slavery was cruel and debilitating, not paternalistic and benign. However, memory can also be utilized for opposite effect. It can be brought to the defense of the master and conjure images of contented slaves and peaceful, prosperous plantations. As Edward Said reminds us, "Memory and its representations touch very significantly upon questions of identity, of nationalism of power and authority."[67] Memory can thus both support and resist the status quo. It can confirm or resist reigning historiographical interpretations.

Memories and memoirs, regardless of their point of view, reveal a great deal about the people doing the remembering and their social world. This is true, as we have seen, whether or not their memory is always reliable, whether or not they are always telling the truth. Memoirs are valuable historical resources precisely because of their subjectivity, because they reveal the way individuals perceive and later recollect the historical moments of their lives. They make these revelations without compromising the complexities and contradictions of both lived and recalled experience, without whitewashing vagaries and falsehoods in the name of a particular conception about what constitutes historical truth. An understanding of historical reality as multiperspectival does not mean that we should not try to separate true from false or individual memories from historical consensus. However, it does mean that we cannot dispense with any of these elements. Historical reality is collectively constituted by the experiences of everyone in a given historical moment, and we must endeavor to understand the total package.

Furthermore, when analyzing memoirs, we must look not only at their content—at what the authors claimed to remember—but also at the language they use to express their recollections. Figurative language has the power to capture a complex social reality to a much greater extent than does unadorned, scholarly prose. We will look at the power that language has to shape our historical understanding in the next chapter.

CHAPTER TWO

Literary Techniques and
Historical Understanding

A WELL-CRAFTED MEMOIR enables the student of history to "refeel" a past moment from a particular point of view. This emotional understanding of a particular historical reality is not merely a cosmetic adornment that adds an element of human interest to our historical understanding. Rather, these emotions are partially constitutive of historical reality. If we want to recapture a past moment accurately, these emotions cannot be dispensed with. Although all memoirs can provide the historian with important access to affective aspects of the inside of a historical moment, it is my contention that some autobiographers are particularly adept at capturing the felt experiences of a past reality. I am referring to autobiographies written by, to borrow Susanna Egan's phrase, "artists—not writers by happenstance."[1] The artful use of literary language and the use of literary devices like irony and metaphor do not merely make a literary memoir a more interesting text to read; these elements actually heighten the author's ability to represent lived experience. The complexity of felt experience simply cannot be as accurately described with literal, nonliterary prose.

In order to explore my claim that artfully constructed memoirs have a particular kind of power to illuminate our historical understanding, we must first begin by reflecting on the language used in literary memoirs. How is it different, and thus more historically revealing, than that used in nonliterary memoirs? Literary memoirs utilize language that is distinct from that employed in popular autobiographies (many of which are ghost-written or collaboratively written) by entertainers, CEOs, politicians, and others who are not skilled, creative writers. Unlike popular autobiography, with its titillating claims to "reveal all" and its unabashed allegiance to the marketplace, each literary memoir is intended to be a work of art as well as a chronicle of a life. Literary memoirs are generally not written exclusively to sell books or to score public relations points (although these might be partial considerations on the part of the author); they are primarily intended to be works of art that will outlive the memoirist. However, we cannot make the distinction between literary and nonliterary memoirs by appeal to the author's motivations alone. After all, some authors no doubt set out to create works of art but write critical failures nonetheless. How do some memoirs become works of art while others do not? Why is something like Vladimir Nabokov's memoir *Speak, Memory* considered literature, whereas Lee Iacocca's coauthored autobiography is not?

According to Terry Eagleton, "literary discourse estranges or alienates ordinary speech, but in doing so, paradoxically, brings us into a fuller, more intimate possession of experience."[2] How does literary language perform such a remarkable feat? It does so, in part, merely by drawing attention to itself as literary language and causing readers to pause, to reflect, and to analyze the content of what they are reading. To merely say that literature causes us to think more carefully about what we read seems at first a fairly unremarkable claim. However, the endeavor, discussed in the previous chapter, both to "rethink" and to "refeel" the thoughts of historical agents is a slow and deliberate process. The more involved we become in analyzing a text, the closer we come to understanding what the text's author thought and how she or he felt.

Autobiographical texts that do not demand intensive reading or inspire interpretive quandaries simply do not allow the reader to identify as closely with the authors of the texts. A literal text may be read quickly and put aside, but a literary text requires the kind of ongoing interaction between author, reader, and text that helps facilitate empathetic reconstruction of past events in the present. This kind of intense interplay is necessary if the historian is to be in a position to understand the complexity of an author's thoughts and, as Collingwood would have it, to rethink those thoughts.

Eagleton's claim that literary language "estranges" everyday speech relies on the assumption that we have a consensus on how ordinary language looks and sounds—for how can something be considered strange without a standardized basis for comparison? Because judgments about what makes language "strange" vary chronologically as well as culturally, we cannot have a set basis for comparison. A line from a Keats sonnet such as "Bright star, would I were steadfast as thou art" immediately draws attention to itself as literature. After all, the poet appears to be addressing a star directly or is addressing a person whom he is comparing to a star, neither of which are common conventions in ordinary speech. However, if we were to pluck out of context a phrase or two of the spare, unadorned prose Hemingway writes, we might not have the sense that what we are reading is literature per se. It quickly becomes clear that to recognize literature by the extent to which it "alienates ordinary speech" is not a foolproof identifier, but it is frequently useful nonetheless. If we compare two representative samples of the same genre side by side when one is widely considered literary and the other is not, we can frequently recognize significant differences in the way language is used. Take Iacocca's and Nabokov's autobiographies as a basis for comparison.

Iacocca's autobiography begins almost conversationally, as if he were answering the question "Where did your family come from?" He answers: "Nicola Iacocca, my father, came to this country in 1902 at the age of twelve—poor, alone, and scared."[3] Because adjective series are more characteristic of written than of spoken language, the use of "poor, alone, and scared" draws attention to the fact that he is writing, rather than speaking. However, the adjectives themselves are unimaginative and as such not particularly descriptive or very literary. The adjectives chosen conform to clichéd, linguistic expectations rather than subverting them. It is also immediately clear that the text we are about to read will follow a formula. Iacocca's autobiography is one of many variations on *the* American story: child of immigrants makes good, pulls himself up by his bootstraps, rises from rages to riches, and so forth. We know the basic plot in its entirety from the very first sentence even without possession of the specific details, and the substance of his life story is quickly revealed in all the complexity it will ever assume.

Contrast this formulaic stab at autobiographical writing with the first sentence of Nabokov's autobiography: "The cradle rocks above the abyss, and common sense tells us that our existence is but a brief crack of light between two eternities and darkness."[4] Without a formula we can quickly recognize, we are caught off guard. Already, from the very first sentence, we know that Nabokov's conception of himself and of the autobiographical act is more complicated than a long list of his accomplishments. We are already told to be aware of the relationship of one individual life to eternity.

We quickly are confronted with what we intuitively already know: from the moment of birth, life is uncertain. Unlike Iacocca, Nabokov captures something of the experiential aspects of living alongside uncertainty. We do not already know all the plot elements that will compose Nabokov's life story. Nabokov's cradle precariously "rocks above an abyss," while the trajectory of Iacocca's life is already clear from the first sentence.

It is immediately obvious that Nabokov's autobiography poses a greater interpretive challenge than Iacocca's, and we can assume that our greater efforts to understand Nabokov's story will have a greater payoff in the form of a richer, more nuanced reconstruction of Nabokov's life. Nabokov capitalizes on the autobiographer's ability to capture, as Popkin tells us, "one of the fundamental characteristics of human experience: the fact that we will end our lives without knowing how our stories will look when they are ended."[5] How can we describe our initial, unreflective understanding that, owing to the literary techniques it utilizes, *Speak, Memory* somehow has more to offer us in our endeavor to understand human nature and to get an insight into the inner workings of one particular life than does Iacocca's autobiography?

Eagleton compares language to the air we breathe. Most of the time we are unaware of it. However, "if the air is suddenly thickened or infected we are forced to attend to our breathing with new vigilance, and the effect of this may be a heightened experience of our bodily life."[6] The same thing is true of language: we suddenly become aware of it when it ceases to function merely to communicate information but is instead transformed into art. On a fairly superficial level, Nabokov's text has a greater impact on us than Iacocca's simply because he succeeds in getting our undivided attention. As we shall see later, once literary memoirists have our attention, they have at their disposal various techniques of literary art that they utilize to give us a complex view of the historical reality of their life.

When we read Iacocca's autobiography, we are not fully aware of the particular language that he is using because it is unremarkable. We might read it absentmindedly on the beach or on an airplane because we are interested in finding out the skeletal facts of his life: his educational background, his tenure at Ford, the business decisions he made while managing Chrysler. We might initially open Nabokov's memoir with the same motivations in mind, but the language Nabokov uses is so evocative, so sensory, so strange that the atmosphere does change. We are no longer halfheartedly leafing through it on the airplane; we are, if we allow it, transported into another realm and are able to enjoy the thrill of "vicarious experience," which Barzun and Graff claim draws people to history. This changed atmosphere is due to the literary merits of the text. Instinctively we read a literary text with a higher state of awareness than when we read a newspaper, a recipe, or a nonliterary memoir. Literature simply demands more from its readers, and readers who actively engage with it receive more for their efforts.

Not only does the aesthetic power of language made strange so change the atmosphere that readers are primed to live vicariously while reading a text, but the more artfully an autobiography is written, the longer and more vividly readers will remember the text and their interaction with it. For example, David Blight has argued that W. E. B. Du Bois made a conscious shift in his work from "social science to art" in large part because Du Bois believed that artfully written prose could convey his message more powerfully. Blight situates himself among "many scholars [who] have stressed the importance of aesthetic appeal in the art of memory." He claims that "the emotional power of a historical image or of an individual or collective memory is what renders it lasting. . . . The more profound the poetic imagery or the metaphoric association, the more lasting a memory might be in any culture."[7] With these criteria in mind, Blight labels Du Bois's classic text *Souls of Black Folk* as a "memory palace . . . of unforgettable images, conveyed with such aesthetic power that readers and writers might return to it, generation after generation, for historical understanding and inspiration."[8]

Literary memoirs are particularly valuable historical resources in large part simply because they form lasting impressions and inspire vivid mental imagery. When images are artfully drawn, they make a lasting impact on the reader's imagination and in the process often become resident false memories in the minds of their readers. If we conceive of history as vicarious experience, it only follows that such experiences should produce memories as well as a deeper subjective understanding of the past. Images from literary memoirs form memory palaces that we add to or subtract from as we learn more about a historical era.

Powerful aesthetic imagery is not confined to formal literature or dependent on the skill of classically educated writers like W. E. B. Du Bois. Robert O'Meally argues that, "more than any other form of human expression, art communicates the excitement as well as the treacherous unpredictability of history's flights."[9] However, the art O'Meally is referring to is primarily vernacular art. Folktales and folksongs might conjure imagery as vivid as that in a work of literature. It is not my intention to draw a distinction between "high" and "low" art but rather to contrast the figurative and artful use of language with the literal and commonplace.

So what techniques do literary artists use that enable their texts to serve as "memory palaces" in the minds of their readers? Interestingly, in describing the difference between reading literature and reading nonliterary writing, Eagleton gives us a clue. He tells us, "Language is like air." His use of a simile demonstrates one of the many techniques of literary writing that enable it to describe a complex social reality better than literal prose. Faced with the difficult task of contrasting literary and nonliterary language, Eagleton chose to describe the difference by means of an effective comparison. Even if his reader had never thought about the distinction before, Eagleton knew that his reader would know what it felt like to be suddenly blasted with humid air or to breathe in smoke or smog. When the air quality is altered, breathing can no longer be taken for granted. Just as we do not notice the quality of air unless it changes, he tells us, we generally do not notice language unless its quality changes, too, and it becomes literature.

Metaphoric language enables authors to describe one thing in the terms of another. Sometimes, as with Eagleton's comparison of literary language and infected air, a metaphor enables an author to explain a difficult concept in terms of a more familiar one. However, this basic definition of the metaphor does not do justice to the power that metaphoric images can have. By grouping often seemingly unrelated objects or concepts, the writer who utilizes metaphor inspires a reconceptualization of the object under comparison. For example, the metaphor "A mighty fortress is our God" conjures up one image of the nature of God, while another metaphor might highlight a different, even contradictory, aspect of God, such as "God is a consuming fire." The more benign image of "God as the baby infant Jesus" characterizes God in yet another way, and each metaphor could be used for a distinctive rhetorical effect and will cause the reader to conceptualize God much differently.

Metaphor, in causing the reader or listener to juxtapose different images and to actively engage in interpretation, is capable of revealing things that literal language cannot. William Franke argues that "the sense of the world must lie beyond the limits of the totality of facts that make up the world and that *can* be articulated in straightforward, fact-stating language saying *how* it is."[10] Metaphor brings to life images that are not literally true but can nonetheless be more revealing about the nature of things than unadorned fact. For example, love is not literally a rose. However, we could argue that the language of fact is far less adept at explaining romantic love than is the single image of a perfect red rose.

Some recent theories of metaphor argue that metaphor is more fundamental than an ornamental figure of speech and that human beings think and structure their experiences through metaphors. Conceptual structure theories of metaphor argue that "linguistic metaphors are not arbitrarily generated through the random contrast of any two conceptual domains, but reflect a constrained set of conceptual mappings, itself metaphorical, that structures our thinking, reasoning, and understanding."[11] According to this theory, humans are able to interpret commonplace metaphors as easily and unthinkingly as literal speech because "metaphoricality [is] a central cognitive mechanism."[12]

Literary metaphors are so powerful precisely because we are hardwired to process information that way. Literary metaphors have a particular impact on us, according to Raymond W. Gibbs, because of "their novel way of articulating some underlying conceptual mapping that already structures part of our experience of the world."[13] Metaphors of this kind do what good literature in general does; as Robert Anchor reminds us, it "fulfill[s] expectations along unexpected lines."[14]

To begin an examination of how figurative language is more evocative than literal language, let's look at the concluding paragraphs of Richard Wright's memoir *Black Boy* as an example. At the conclusion of the autobiography, Wright has decided to leave the Communist Party and to continue fighting against racial injustice as a politically independent writer. His first move will be to write his own life story. In straightforward, nonliterary prose, Wright might write a sentence summarizing his intentions much as I just have. He might say, "I will write my autobiography and examine the question of racial injustice in the process." Instead he writes:

> I wanted to try to build a bridge of words between me and the world
> outside, that world which was so distant and elusive that it seemed unreal.
>   I would hurl words into the darkness and wait for an echo, and if an
> echo sounded, no matter how faintly, I would send other words to tell, to

march, to fight, to create a sense of hunger for life that gnaws in us all, to keep alive in our hearts a sense of the inexpressibly human.[15]

The net impact of Wright's closing lines of *Black Boy*, because of the literary language he chooses, is much greater than what would have been achieved if the same information had been conveyed in summary or in a nonliterary fashion. In fact, the disparity between the nonliterary summary "I will write an autobiography that expresses what it is to be human" and what Wright actually says is such that Wright's feelings can be conveyed *only* by using the techniques of literary art.

Not only does Wright communicate the basic information that he has decided to devote his life to writing, but he also sheds light on the hardships inherent in the writing life. He is aware of the difficulties in using language to represent the reality of his life and thus compares writing to building a bridge. Wright is aware of the distance between his lived experience and its retelling as described in the pages of an autobiography. Although his goal is to paint so vivid a picture of life in the Jim Crow South that his readers will be forced to experience it vicariously, with or without their consent, he knows that there is necessarily a gulf between reality and representations of it. By coming clean with the problem of representation, he is asking his reader to collaborate with him to bridge the gaps between their present reality, Wright's past reality, and the language Wright enlists to describe it.

He makes a startling language choice when he tells us that he will "hurl" (like a grenade?) words into a potentially unfriendly world. This somewhat violent imagery stands in direct contrast to images of a cloistered intellectual stolidly writing in an isolated corner of a library. He personifies and then deputizes language, ordering it "to tell, to march, to fight." The description of words as soldiers quickly and economically conveys a great deal to the reader. We are shown how difficult the life of the writer, any writer, is. It is so difficult to find the right words that writing is a lot like warfare. Even more significant, Wright's description of words as soldiers also reminds us of the brutal realities of the Jim Crow South. In giving voice to nameless "black boys" throughout the South and in asserting their humanity, Wright is fighting an uphill battle. He is not writing to a receptive or even disinterested audience. He is writing to a nation steeped in institutionalized and legalized racism, and many members of this audience are hostile to his autobiographical efforts before they have read the first sentence. He will indeed have to "hurl" language at people who would rather not listen to him.

None of the complexity of what he is saying could have been conveyed had he chosen to write straightforward, literal prose. He might have painstakingly and longwindedly written a treatise on representation and on the craft of writing fiction. He might also have inserted one final denouncement of racism. Instead he leaves us with the imagery of words as soldiers and in so doing captures the difficulties of his undertaking while reminding us of the precarious position he is in. As a black writer he does not have the luxury of being only a writer. He must also be a soldier, and his words his weapons.

As we can see from this brief examination of the conclusion of *Black Boy*, Wright's use of metaphoric language conveys a complexity of meaning that could not have been conveyed without using figurative language. Similarly, literary artists have at their disposal the tool of irony, which can also be used to convey many levels of meaning. Irony can take various forms. The earliest use of the concept is found in Plato, where we are introduced to Socratic irony. In Plato's dialogues, Socrates feigns ignorance and asks seemingly naive questions in order ultimately to expose the true ignorance of his interlocutors. Plato and his readers are aware of the ironic situation because they know that it is Socrates' questioners who are ignorant, not Socrates himself. Irony is also expressed when one says something one does not mean. In speech, this kind of ironic meaning is often indicated by the inflection with which it is spoken. For example, it would be ironic to see a forty-dollar hamburger listed on a menu at a fancy Manhattan restaurant and to declare, after a sharp intake of breath, "That's quite a bargain!" Situations can be ironic as well. For example, it would be ironic if a soldier lived through a war only to be hit and killed by a car immediately after his or her tour of duty was over. Regardless of the form it takes, irony generally involves a tension between the way things appear to be (or should be) and they way they really are. In order to be effective, Socratic or dramatic irony also relies on the existence of two different audiences, a superficial audience, which is aware of the surface meaning, and a true audience, which is aware of the true meaning of the words or situation.

Irony is often used in literary memoirs to great effect. For example, consider the wedding scene in Carolyn Briggs's memoir *This Dark World*. Briggs is describing her wedding. She is eighteen years old and pregnant.

Out of obligation and necessity, she is marrying her first boyfriend, an awkward nineteen-year-old with no real job prospects, and is pushing aside dreams of college to take up a life of poverty and motherhood in a tiny trailer park in the middle of Iowa. However, despite the unhappiness surrounding the event, all the trappings of a happy wedding are present: flowers, expensive new clothes, cake and punch. Briggs writes, "My father in cowboy boots and I in my dotted swiss approached the altar. My bridesmaids, Lisa and Katherine, waited tearfully for me, wearing lavender dresses and carrying yellow roses."[16] From the perspectives of Lisa and Katherine, the tears they were crying were tears of happiness. They were caught up in the appearances of a happy wedding and not in tune with the grim significance this ceremony had in the life of their friend. However, Briggs, her parents, and the readers of the memoir constitute a true audience, which is not fooled by the yellow roses and the silk dresses. For them this wedding was an unhappy occasion; for them the bridesmaids' tears were tears of sadness. Here appearance and reality are at odds. Weddings should be happy, and bridesmaids should (if they cry at all) cry tears of joy. Briggs, when confronted with the carefully constructed artifice of a joyful union, is able to catch a glimpse of what her wedding day *should* have been like and to compare that vision with her present situation. If Briggs had not chosen to highlight the irony of an unhappy wedding, she could not have as accurately conveyed what it felt like to be an eighteen-year-old pregnant bride embarking on a life she did not choose. The melancholy nature of her situation is highlighted in contrast to the image of what a wedding should be.

Robert Paul Wolff provocatively argues that there are certain concepts that can be conveyed only ironically. He uses the example of a lapsed Catholic who now considers herself an atheist. How should this person answer if asked whether she currently believes in God? The answer "yes" is obviously inaccurate, since she now considers herself an atheist. However, the word "no" does not accurately convey her true convictions either if she, like many formerly religious people, still maintains in one part of herself a shred of superstition that indeed there is a God. To answer "I once believed in God, but I do not now" would also be an inaccurate answer that would deny part of her true feelings and would also dismiss the profound impact her Catholicism and her onetime belief in God have had on the person she currently is. In order to describe her true feelings succinctly, Wolff suggests, she might "reply—employing, ever so faintly exaggeratedly, the singsong tone of the Apostles' Creed—'I believe in God the Father Almighty Creator of Heaven and Earth and in Jesus Christ.'" This ironic voice would convey to a true audience that she grew up in the Catholic faith and is no longer among the faithful but still bears the imprint of her time in the church. Wolff argues: "If the speaking self is complex, many-layered, capable of reflection, self-deception, ambivalence, of unconscious thought processes, of projections, interjections, displacements, transferences, and all manner of ambiguities—in short, if the *history* of the self is directly present as part of its current nature—then only a language containing within itself the literary resources corresponding to these complexities will suffice to speak the truth."[17]

Willie Morris, a white Mississippian by birth who moved north both physically and metaphorically as he tried to conquer his native racism, describes the same kind of tension between a former self and a current self that Wolff's lapsed Catholic experienced. In his memoir *North Toward Home*, Morris describes a day in the mid-1960s that he spends in Manhattan with two other transplanted southerners, the novelist William Styron and the historian C. Vann Woodward. The three men spend the day giving radio interviews about the South and their feelings about the civil rights movement. They are cast as enlightened, white southerners who are speaking to similarly enlightened northerners and Canadians (a scenario that Morris negates elsewhere by talking about the virulent racism he has encountered in New York). At lunch Woodward tells his friends about witnessing the March on Montgomery and in so doing vividly describes the "red-necks" who come out in droves to oppose Martin Luther King Jr. Woodward confesses, "And I'll have to admit something. A little part of me was there with 'em."

As the men are leaving the restaurant, Styron and Morris lag behind Woodward, who is forced to wait for them on the other side of a busy intersection. Woodward shouts, "You're the slowest country boys I ever saw."[18] Woodward is jovially complaining because his companions are literally lagging behind, but, perhaps unwittingly, he is also impatient with himself. He has spent the day talking about books, giving interviews, and drinking martinis in Manhattan, but part of him is still a "country boy" who was socialized as a southerner and a racist, try as he might to suppress that aspect of his former self. C. Vann Woodward may have written *The*

Strange Career of Jim Crow to expose the roots of institutionalized racism, but the rational part of him, which could analyze and condemn southern injustice, must coexist with the part of him that grew up under its tyranny, the part of him that could momentarily identify with the outspoken racists out to stop Dr. King. The gap between the person he is and the person that he would like to be is revealed in the characterization of his friends (and by extension himself) as slow country boys who, despite their fame and their sophisticated lifestyles, are unable to escape their roots completely.

When memoirists effectively utilize irony, it enhances our historical understanding of a particular era because human interactions contain layers of meanings, some of which are competing. A literal rendering of a historical moment cannot possibly convey the true complexity of the moment precisely because different historical agents understand and experience each moment differently. The presence of layered meanings, this disjuncture between how a situation appears to one participant and how it appears another, is itself a form of irony that can be explained only by use of literary techniques.

Irony has been a particularly useful tool for literary memoirists who have tried to capture the complexity of American race relations. For example, memoirists who have described life in the segregated American South are writing about a social situation fraught with irony. Because southern conventions demanded outward subservience from African Americans regardless of their personal feelings, any interaction between a white southerner and black southerner might be weighted with irony. White southerners expected cheerful deference, and African Americans who did not exhibit the right attitude might be watched with suspicion, labeled "uppity," and fired from their job. Because of this expectation and the grim consequences if it was not met, black southerners might answer questions such as "Are you happy working for me?" with an exaggerated smile and an emphatic "Yes, sir." While the requisite responses delivered in the requisite fashion might satisfy whites who wanted to reassure themselves about the contentment of their black employees, an African American listener overhearing the same exchange would interpret the energetically proffered "Yes, sir" differently. The African American primary audience would understand that the put-upon black employee meant the opposite of what she or he was forced to say.

These Jim Crow interactions between black and whites were twentieth-century incarnations of earlier dealings between masters and slaves. Slaves would sing spirituals that the masters interpreted as purely religious songs but that the slaves knew were cries for freedom in this world. Slaves also told folktales that were outwardly about mischievous animals but had another layer of meaning where the animals enacted master-slave relationships in which the slaves came out on top.

Because so many of the black and white relationships in the Jim Crow South were laden with irony, an accurate portrayal of that era would have to convey this crucial aspect of social interactions. Literal depictions of southern race relations that do not capture irony cannot capture a primary aspect of the social reality of that time. Every interaction between a black and white southerner contained layers of meanings. The outward reenactment of prescribed social roles camouflaged but could not erase deeper meanings. White southerners, if they allowed themselves, knew that black southerners could not be as content as they pretended, and black southerners learned to perform the societal script they were handed without really meaning it. A work of literary art that utilizes irony can capture this complex reality and these layered meanings.

Not only can skillful literary memoirists utilize metaphors and irony to represent their complex historical experiences convincingly, but they also have the ability to bridge the gap between their particular historical experiences and those of the reader who comes to the text from a completely different historical situation. Let us return for a moment to the final paragraph of *Black Boy*, where Wright attempts to universalize his experiences in this way. Although the main goal of the memoir is to indict southern racism, he also wants to use his writing to convey "the inexpressibly human." Thus *Black Boy*, like all literary memoirs, is simultaneously particular and universal. It can be read as a historical resource that allows us to come to a greater understanding of Jim Crow, but it is also applicable to other times and other contexts. Literary memoirs are allegorical—that is, they have more than one level of meaning. According to E. D. Hirsch Jr., "such writing typically intends to convey meaning beyond its immediate occasion into a future context which is very different from that of its production. . . . Authors of such future-oriented writings intend to make them applicable to (in other words, allegorizable to) unforeseen situations."[19]

Good ethnography, like literature, is also allegorical, according to cultural anthropologist James Clifford: "A recognition of allegory emphasizes the fact that realistic portraits, to the extent that they are 'convincing' or 'rich,' are extended metaphors, patterns of associations that point to coherent (theoretical, esthetic, moral) additional meanings."[20] An understanding of ethnography as allegory allows Clifford to interpret a scene from Marjorie Shostak's book *Nisa: The Life and Words of a !Kung Woman* on two different levels. The passage Clifford analyzes recounts Nisa giving birth alone in the bush, but on another level Clifford reads it as "an allegory of (female) humanity."[21] Similarly, *Black Boy* can be read simultaneously as Richard Wright's memoir, as the story of all "black boys" in the Jim Crow South, and also as an allegory of all human oppression. Wright's ability to universalize his experience makes his life story resonate with his readers. By claiming to convey "the inexpressibly human" and elevating his own experiences from the particular to the universal, he challenges the potential apathy of his readers, reminding them that his story also belongs to them, to all of us.

Students of history are better able to refeel the past experiences of Wright or any other historical agent if they can draw on their own emotions and feelings to help them. Because literary memoirs are universal as well as particular, historians cannot help but find aspects of the lives chronicled that resonate with aspects their own, and they can draw on those similarities to achieve a greater historical understanding. "Why," Hirsch asks rhetorically, "should anyone be interested in a story that lacks analogical applications to his or her own experience?"[22] Although it would seem harsh and narrow minded to categorically declare that all nonliterary memoirs are uninteresting, it is generally true that the allegorical and universal aspects of great literature enable its readers to identify more closely with it than with nonliterary texts.

So far in our attempt to come to terms with what makes the literary memoir a particularly good historical resource, we have discussed its ability to gain the readers' undivided attention, its effectiveness in inspiring lasting mental images in the minds of its readers, its use of metaphors and irony to convey concepts that cannot be expressed through literal speech, and its allegorical qualities that make it relevant to any time and any place. Although all these characteristics make the literary memoir a potentially powerful and highly descriptive text, all of them could be equally true of a novel. What kind of insights can the literary memoir give us, if any, that a novel cannot?

Of course, as discussed in the previous chapter, a literary memoir is historically significant because, unlike the novel, it is based in fact and refers to a real past rather than to a fictional world. Because of this the memoir can give us facts, which are literally verifiable, as well as insights into the way the historical reality it recounts was structured. Novels, like the works of Dickens, might give us revealing glimpses of what life was like during the historical period they are set in, but they are not intended to be literally verifiable. Memoirs, despite the myriad ways in which they might stretch, evade, or incorrectly portray the truth, are grounded in real people, places, and things and thus are better suited to tell us "what really happened" than are fictional texts.

However, even though they are rooted in fact, literary memoirs also are free to utilize the techniques of fiction. Because literary memoirists are skilled writers, they are experienced at creating fictional worlds, and they bring their expertise to bear when describing the real one. Because they literally write the fictional world into being, authors of fictional texts have a godlike perspective over the text. The talented creative writer knows how to describe a fictional world in all its complexity: to capture the interpersonal relationships between characters that inhabit that world and to describe vividly what that fictional world looks like, sounds like, and smells like. Creative writers bring this same set of skills with them when they turn to autobiography, and the result is often a description of the real world that is as detailed and as revealing as that found in a finely crafted novel.

Literary memoirists, when they write autobiography, essentially transform themselves into characters and then describe the world as it exists from these characters' point of view. This is not something a historian of a particular time period can do, for historians must write narratives that describe a world that simply does not exist from their personal point of view. Historians write about vanished worlds. Since historians are not characters in the historical worlds they describe, they cannot be expected to have the same kinds of insights that an inhabitant of that world would have. Historians cannot capture the immediacy of past experience the way a literary memoirist can. They write about fixed but arbitrary chronological divisions. Historians pick beginning and ending dates when they write histories of an era, and these dates are imbued with a great historical significance, often the beginning or ending of a war, the election of a political leader, or the start or close of economic catastrophe or unusual prosperity. Real life does not have this same kind of structure. Robert Anchor claims that one of the realist writers' goals is to be able to "produce and sustain a sense of the openness of history within the closed circle of narrative."[23] The literary memoirist is frequently able to capture a sense of the chance, the possibility, and the arbitrariness of life in a way that a historian cannot. Memoirists are able to capture this sense of openness because they are familiar with the uncertainty they felt at various stages in their life and at various points in history, whereas the historian always knows the outcome.

Literary memoirists also give us important clues as to the way they and others like them may have conceptualized their world. Each memoirist reveals a great deal about his or her society simply by means of the language he or she uses. As David Harlan argues, "By studying the conceptual language of a particular culture, we could learn what it was or was not possible for people in that culture to have thought."[24] When we read memoirs written in periods of time other than our own, it quickly becomes clear that the operating assumptions about what is possible, desirable, good, and conceivable vary greatly from era to era. According to J. G. A. Pocock, the historian must "point out conventions and regularities that indicate what could and could not be spoken in the language, and in what ways the language *qua* paradigm encouraged, obliged, or forbade its users to speak and think."[25]

If we return once again to the example of memoirs written about life in the segregated American South in the first half of the twentieth century, we see that the way the issue of race is talked about is a prime example of the way the conceptual language of a particular culture can dictate what kind of conversations can take place. In memoirs by many white southerners, racism is taken for granted. The southern caste system is so much a part of the world the memoirist inhabits that she or he cannot think her or his way outside that system. In contrast, African American memoirs and memoirs written by whites politically opposed to the southern way of life deliberately challenge the conceptual language of their culture, which legitimates racism. These memoirs attempt to redefine the way society thinks about race by transforming the way it is spoken of. However, even when memoirists make efforts to transcend the language about race available to them, it often becomes clear that they are more influenced by the conceptual language of their times than they would like to think.

Lillian Smith's memoir *Killers of the Dream* was written to fight racism and to describe the socialization of southern racists. Nonetheless, as we will discuss in chapter 4, Smith's text unwittingly bears the imprint of the racial thinking of her time. She maintains essentialist ideas about racial differences, referring to the "biologically rooted humor" of southern mammies and claiming that all slaves possessed "a marvelous love of life and play, a physical grace and rhythm and a pyschosexual vigor."[26] Although Smith calls on what she believes are positive stereotypes to counteract the racism of her day, they are stereotypes nonetheless. The fact that Smith was able to overcome her socialization as a white racist and to actively fight against the southern caste system is remarkable. However, her belief in innate racial differences demonstrates that, despite her ability to transcend the grossest manifestations of the racism of her society, even she could not completely break free of the conceptual framework of her time. Thus, often in spite of themselves, memoirs give us a glimpse into some of the deeply embedded assumptions of a particular society.

All texts, not just literary ones, reveal aspects of the conceptual language of a particular culture. We can also get insights about the structure of the world from diaries, letters, and more public kinds of writing as well. The use of language that is culturally revealing in memoirs and in other kinds of writing is generally unwitting. Writers utilize the language that is available to them. However, sometimes literary memoirists use their skills as writers to give us more deliberate clues about the prevailing conceptual structure of the world they inhabit.

Literary texts can reveal important things about the nature of the social world that other texts cannot. Skilled, creative writers are able to give us important clues about the shape of their conceptual world by the use of repeated symbols or words. Literary memoirists might deliberately give certain words, phrases, or images a charged significance in their memoir in order to emphasize the significance these ideas had in their own life. Whenever one of these words or phrases appears in the text, it is designed to evoke a certain set of associations about the memoirist's own subjective experience. Because daily living is continually impacted by the way, on a symbolic level, the social world is structured, the use of these evocative words and phrases conveys something important about lived experience. Powerful symbols often resonate through an entire culture and influence politics, specific events, and social behavior in ways that we cannot hope to understand without a comprehension of the pervasiveness of these symbols.

In Jim Crow memoirs, particularly those written by white southern-ers, repeated references to geographical space reveal a great deal about the southern worldview. Southern novelist Eudora Welty famously waxed po-etic about the importance of a "sense of place" in all fiction writing.[27] Both she and her fellow Mississippian William Faulkner produced fiction rooted in a belief in southern distinctiveness, which could be secured only in op-position to the North. Harry Crews, too, shared this southern fascination with geographical space, as revealed by his memoir's subtitle, "The Biogra-phy of a Place." Sometimes this North/South opposition is accompanied by feelings of southern inferiority, with some southerners feeling marginal-ized as inhabitants of an intellectual backwoods, H. L. Mencken's "Sahara of the Bozart." William Howarth claims that when people "speak of going *up* north and *down* south" they are often implying a "vertical scale of val-ues."[28] Intellectual curiosity and a repugnance for institutionalized racism led southern memoirist Willie Morris to repudiate the South and, upon graduation from college, to head "North Toward Home," as the title of his memoir reveals. Other southern memoirists have proclaimed hostility toward the North and asserted southern superiority. William Alexander Percy, author of *Lanterns on the Levee*, matter-of-factly proclaimed, "The North destroyed my South."[29]

Others become most aware of the significance of the North/South di-chotomy only after traveling north. Faulkner depicts this situation fictively in *Absalom, Absalom!* when Quentin Compson's Harvard roommate asks him why he hates the South. " 'I dont hate it,' Quentin said, quickly, at once, immediately; 'I dont hate it,' he said. *I dont hate it* he thought, pant-ing in the cold air, the iron New England dark: *I dont. I dont! I dont hate it! I dont hate it!*" Compson's defensiveness reveals his ambivalent feelings about the South and how out of place his southernness seemed in a different geo-graphical space. In an autobiographical essay, J. Bill Berry remembered his own experience of leaving Fayetteville, Arkansas, to attend graduate school at Princeton University in 1967. Upon his arrival at the campus, he imme-diately met a fellow southerner, whose "accent filled the air with molasses." His fellow southerner declares, "You're going to hate it here."[30] Berry re-called that transplanted southerners at Princeton chose either to assimilate and deny their roots (one Mississippian even went so far as to acquire a fake British accent) or to embrace the South and risk being stigmatized as different. Berry remembered an incident in which a Princeton anthropology student asked him what it was like to grow up in Arkansas. After answering her, he realized that "[he] was . . . her very first Samoan."[31] The juxtaposition of North and South not only influenced his perception of himself and his region but also colored other people's perceptions of him.

Regardless of the context, the contrast between North and South and the symbolic significance of living "down south" imply a feeling of difference in southern memoirs. Sometimes these feelings take the form of regional pride; at other times they take the shape of southern inferiority complexes. Whenever the North is mentioned in Jim Crow memoirs, it is accompanied by a complex set of sometimes contradictory associations. It represents freedom (both political and intellectual) to some and tyranny to others. It is both culturally enlightened and morally bankrupt. It is everything the South is not, for good or for bad. It is the yardstick that the South must measure itself by; Jim Crow southerners, particularly those who were well read or well traveled, were aware of the South's status as a region set apart. Repeated geographical references in southern memoirs highlight this feeling of difference and demonstrate how a southern identity (in contrast to a northern one), whether construed positively or negatively, impacted the way memoirists saw their world and their place in it. The South lived in opposition to and in the shadow of the North, and this idea is represented by repeated geographical references in southern autobiography.

References to segregated spaces also are of great significance in Jim Crow memoirs. These allusions are, for obvious reasons, particularly pervasive in African American autobiography but are present in white memoirs as well. References to separate facilities for African American and white southerners demonstrate not only the way the nation was divided between North and South but also the way the South was divided against itself. Maya Angelou captures the impact of segregated spaces on her psyche by comparing herself to a "caged bird" in her first memoir, *I Know Why the Caged Bird Sings*. The pervasive imagery of forbidden geographical spaces where black southerners cannot enter also highlights the anxiety southerners felt about the simultaneous distance and propinquity of whites and blacks. Interaction between the races was necessary, and often mutually desirable, but in some contexts it was taboo. Lillian Smith shows that the metaphor of racial segregation was so pervasive that it could be used in other contexts as well. She claims that all southerners learned that "parts of your body are segregated areas which you must stay away from and keep others away from. These areas you touch only when necessary. In other words, you cannot associate freely with them any more than you can associate freely with colored children."[32]

By artfully and deliberately making references to geographical spaces—both in terms of a North/South dichotomy and in terms of segregated spaces—southern memoirists reveal to their readers something important about the southern psyche. Wherever Jim Crow southerners went, whatever Jim Crow southerners did, they were accompanied by a feeling of difference. They were southerners, not northerners; they were either white or black. These differences could make southerners feel either inferior or superior. They might make them feel angry or content, vulnerable or safe. They might also physically inhibit where southerners could go, in terms of segregated spaces. As a consequence, these geographies had a profound impact on both southerners' daily life and how they conceptualized themselves. Skilled, creative writers can capture this reality by constantly reminding their readers—in myriad, sometimes subtle, ways—that these geographies influenced every other aspect of life. To be a southerner meant living "down south." It also meant using particular restrooms and drinking fountains. The significance of these locations, however, transcended the physical everyday reality of where one lived and where one went. They took on a greater significance, also influencing how southerners saw themselves and their world.

The creative writer's use of symbols, literary language, irony, metaphors, and allegory enables her or him to describe more accurately how a complex historical reality looked, smelled, sounded, and felt. A novelist can capture these same sensations, but unlike a memoir, a novel is not rooted in real people, places, and events and thus cannot make literal truth claims. Our historical insights are enriched by the efforts of realist novelists to capture aspects of a particular social reality artfully. However, despite the valuable insights provided by fiction writers, they do not write about a real world, a world that exists outside the text. This epistemological distinction is crucial. Literary memoirists are able to draw on the same tools that are available to writers of fiction, but they use them to describe real people, real places, and real events.

In the next three chapters, I look closely at several literary memoirs written about life in the segregated South. I demonstrate ways that the historical study of memoirs can enrich our understanding of this particular time period. The skillful memoirists discussed in this book used their considerable talents to describe complex, multifaceted Jim Crow experiences that share certain similarities but remain quite distinctive nonetheless. Read together, these autobiographies reveal that there was no singular Jim Crow history or representative experience.

CHAPTER THREE

African American Memoirists Remember Jim Crow

RICHARD WRIGHT'S *Black Boy: A Record of Childhood and Youth* (1945) is perhaps the most widely read and certainly the most commented-on memoir of the African American Jim Crow experience.[1] Wright portrays life in the Jim Crow South as unremittingly bleak and as characterized by poverty, violence, and anxiety as well as by a spirit of anti-intellectualism that Wright found just as oppressive as the economic deprivation of his childhood. Protest is at the center of Wright's autobiographical writing just as it is in his fiction. *Black Boy* is a literary rendering of great anger, with a depiction of life so grim that many have questioned Wright's veracity as a result.

In contrast, Zora Neale Hurston, Wright's contemporary, sidesteps protest altogether in her Jim Crow autobiography *Dust Tracks on a Road* (1942). She infamously declares that she is "not conscious of [her] race no matter where [she might] go," thereby confounding many of her readers unable to believe that such a lack of race consciousness could be feasible, particularly during the dismal political climate of Hurston's day.[2]

Henry Louis Gates Jr.'s memoir *Colored People* (1994) contains echoes of both Wright and Hurston. Overall, Gates's Jim Crow experiences are more similar to those of Hurston as he celebrates black culture and minimizes, to the extent possible, racism. Unlike his predecessors, Gates recalls the twilight years of Jim Crow. Despite coming of age decades later than Wright and Hurston, Gates was all too familiar with many of the peculiarities of the southern caste system. However, Gates also lived to see some aspects of the system of racial preference dismantled. For example, he attended integrated schools, and his recollections of Jim Crow bear the imprint of his much different experience.

Richard Wright, *Black Boy*

In *Black Boy* Wright describes growing up in Mississippi and Arkansas, telling a now familiar story about segregation and poverty in the rural South during the early decades of the twentieth century. However, he narrates not only the nuts and bolts of his lived experiences—what actually happened to him—but also the emotional aspects of growing up under such limited circumstances. Wright's emotional responses, his fear and anger, are as much a part of the social reality of Jim Crow as the events of his day. When gauging the impact of the injustices of the southern caste system on his personal development, Wright recalls, "Nothing challenged the totality of my personality so much as this pressure of hate and threat that stemmed from the invisible whites."[3] Wright's characterization of whites as "invisible" is curious and stands in direct contrast to the kind of observations that historians make about the Jim Crow era. Historical writing frequently must concentrate on action, events, concrete happenings, in essence on whatever is "visible" to the historian.

For Wright, one part of Jim Crow reality is the concrete, the visible, what happened to him and to people he knew. He encountered overt white violence. He knew people who were beaten or lynched. He recounts numerous humiliating interactions with white people when he was injured, insulted, and belittled. He attended segregated schools and lived in all-black neighborhoods. As recorded in the text, neither he nor anyone in his family participated in southern politics. Thus he documents concrete experiences with the segregation, racism, and disenfranchisement that are characteristic of Jim Crow in much historical work.

However, another part of his Jim Crow reality, the part that historians cannot as effectively capture, is the way Jim Crow made him feel, the psychological impact of white hatred and the unpredictability of white violence even when he was not bearing the brunt of it. In fact, before young Richard was old enough to look for an after-school job, he had very few direct interactions with the white world. As a small child, the reality of white oppression existed for him only in rumor and innuendo. However, he demonstrates repeatedly that anxiety stemming from "invisible whites" impacted every aspect of his life even when there were no white people around. He tells us: "The things that influenced my conduct as a Negro did not have to happen to me directly; I needed but to hear of them to feel their full effects in the deepest layers of my consciousness. Indeed, the white brutality that I had not seen was a more effective control of my behavior than that which I knew" (172).

This passage and other testimony throughout the text yield important information about the reality of Jim Crow. Wright repeatedly reminds his readers that the threat of white violence accompanied him during every moment of every day. It was there when he attended his segregated school in the morning. A "dread of white people came to live permanently in [his] feelings and imagination" (73). It was there in family interactions. Wright's mother became irritated when he quizzed her about the white world. He sensed her anxiety and was aware that he was being "shut out of the secret, the thing, the reality [he] felt somewhere beneath the words and sentences" (47). The anxiety accompanied him when he was hanging out on the street corner with friends his own age. The "touchstone of fraternity" between Wright and his peers was the level of hostility that they could express about white people. This hatred of whites was a natural outgrowth of the constant state of anxiety in which Wright lived (78).

Returning to Collingwood, we remember that each historical moment is composed of an outside and an inside. Wright's discussion of "invisible whites" gives us insight into his felt experience, the inside of his historical moment. His felt experience of Jim Crow was impacted both by the things that happened to him directly and by the idea that something could happen at any moment, the constant threat posed by the invisible white world. Historians who strive to capture the inside of a historical moment without benefit of direct testimony from historical actors must do so imaginatively as they attempt to rethink and refeel from the perspective of a historical actor. Through the memoir, Wright offers his readers unmediated access to the inside aspects of his historical reality. Unlike the historian who tries to re-create Wright's experiences, Wright need not imagine what he thought or how he felt. Instead, Wright's task, using the vehicle of literary art, is to memorably convey those thoughts and feelings.

Even when Wright attempts to capture some pleasant recollections from his childhood, his memories are permeated by his ever present state of apprehension. The book's opening incident sets the tone of violence and fear that characterizes Wright's entire autobiography. As a four-year-old, while playing with fire, Wright set his grandparents' Natchez home ablaze and then hid under the burning house in an attempt to avoid being punished.

Acting out of rage and fear, Wright's mother savagely beat him after discovering his hiding place. After recounting this event, with Wright claiming that his mother nearly killed him, he abruptly switches moods with a lyrical passage about the pleasures of rural life. Evocatively and poetically he describes how his physical environment looked, felt, and tasted. He catalogs twenty-three different sense impressions inspired by the rural Mississippi of his childhood. For example, among other things, he remembers:

> There was the wonder I felt when I first saw a brace of mountainlike, spotted, black and white horses clopping down a dusty road through powdered clay.
> There was the delight I caught in seeing long straight rows of red and green vegetables stretching away in the sun to the bright horizon.
> There was the faint, cool kiss of sensuality when dew came on to my cheeks and shins as I ran down the wet green garden paths in early morning. . . .
> There was the hint of cosmic cruelty that I felt when I saw the curved timbers of a wooden shack that had been warped in the summer sun.
> There was the saliva that formed in my mouth when I smelt clay dust potted with fresh rain.
> There was the cloudy notion of hunger when I breathed the odor of new-cut, bleeding grass.
> And there was the quiet terror that suffused my senses when vast hazes of gold washed earthward from star-heavy skies on silent nights. (7–9)

His recollections of "the faint, cool kiss of sensuality when dew came on to my cheeks and shins" and "the aching glory in masses of clouds burning gold and purple from an invisible sun" are unambiguously positive, the kind of nostalgic associations one would expect autobiographers to have about their birthplace (7–8). He uses the words "delight" and "love" and "nostalgia" to describe the physical world. However, these images, from one of the few passages in the book in which Wright ascribes childlike wonder or joy to his younger self, are punctuated by the violent imagery of "watching a chicken leap about blindly after its neck had been broken" and "the speechless astonishment of seeing a hog stabbed through the heart" (7–8). Even these, his most positive associations from his youth, are interrupted by startling word choices. The natural world also inspires associations with "hunger," "hot panic," and "quiet terror." Included in this list of sense impressions is the "the hint of cosmic cruelty that [he] felt when [he] saw the curved timbers of a wooden shack that had been warped in the summer sun." We see here a dim, childlike awareness of the consequences of the southern caste system as he looks at what may be a sharecropper's cabin, perhaps even his earliest home, and sees signs of poverty and the toll that the harsh environment has taken. He already vaguely knows that the universe is unfair. Thus even when Wright tries to recall positive associations from his childhood, he quickly returns to the imagery of violence and fear, demonstrating that anxiety about the hostile white world permeated every aspect of his waking life.

This passage from *Black Boy* reveals one of the unique historical insights the literary memoir can give us. Wright lulls us with idyllic descriptions of rural southern life only to jar us later with his use of surprisingly dark descriptive words that seem out of place. The most positive recollections, characterized by "love," "delight," "sensuality," and "nostalgia," are at the beginning of the list. His emotive responses to his environment become progressively more ambiguous. Finally the reader is left with the image of a warped shack. Wright recalls being filled with a "cloudy notion of hunger" when he smelled newly cut grass and being overcome with "quiet terror" as he looked at the sky. Readers are able to experience these things as Wright did as they imaginatively scan his environment and follow his stream of consciousness. The tone of hunger and terror with which he ends the passage is amplified throughout the rest of the text. When he surveys his landscape, his thoughts are laden with myriad associations. For Wright, the natural world reflects some of the tensions present in the social world. No doubt a white southerner surveying the same landscape would entertain a different set of associations. To Wright, or any other social agent, no object, natural or otherwise, is innocent or can be surveyed outside personal perceptions.

In *Black Boy* Wright powerfully coaxes his reader into refeeling life as an African American living in Jim Crow, not just during the dramatic moments, in interactions with white racists such as when his family was forced to flee from murderous whites in the middle of the night, but also in day-to-day life. When describing sunsets, the sounds of leaves rustling, the "regality of tall, moss-clad oaks," and so on in the brief passage devoted to describing his environment, Wright demonstrates that he was not immune to childlike wonder. Despite the hardships of his life, he was still aware of beauty and still, as a small child, filled with hope. However, the language in that same passage also reminds the reader that Wright lived in a constant state of anxiety. In recounting tranquil, positive associations he unexpectedly interjects phrases such as "liquid alarm" and "quiet terror" to remind us that all is not well. His Jim Crow experience is a total experience. He cannot compartmentalize the anxiety and anger that he feels and manifest it only when interacting directly with southern whites. It accompanies him everywhere he goes. Using the vehicle of literary art, he captures the uncertainty and fear of his life by using the language of dread and apprehension even in unexpected places.

Wright achieves a similar effect through his use of "hunger" as a metaphor to describe not only his physical state but also his emotional condition. Wright recalls:

> Hunger stole upon me so slowly that at first I was not aware of what hunger really meant. Hunger had always been more or less at my elbow when I played, but now I began to wake up at night to find hunger standing at my bedside, staring at me gauntly. The hunger I had known before this had been no grim, hostile stranger; it had been a normal hunger that had made me beg constantly for bread, and when I ate a crust or two I was satisfied. But this new hunger baffled me, scared me, made me angry and insistent. (14)

Wright is referring here to physical hunger. His father had recently abandoned his mother, leaving the family without money or food. His description of deep and abiding hunger is gripping and yields powerful insights about the dire economic conditions many African Americans found themselves in from time to time after the loss of an income, no matter how meager. The fact that Wright's mother did not have a crust of bread to feed her children or anyone to turn to for help reveals very succinctly how little southern states cared for the physical welfare of their black citizens. The aesthetic power of Wright's language, his personification of hunger as a "hostile stranger," better facilitates a reader's ability to refeel Wright's hunger and desperation.

However, Wright's hunger has another dimension as well. This is hinted at in a conversation with his mother in which he is begging for food:

> "Mama, I'm hungry," I complained one afternoon.
> "Jump up and catch a kungry," she said, trying to make me laugh and forget.

"What's a *kungry*?"

"It's what little boys eat when they get hungry," she said.

"What does it taste like?"

"I don't know."

"Then why do you tell me to catch one?"

"Because you said that you were hungry," she said, smiling.

I sensed that she was teasing me and it made me angry. (15)

In this scene, Wright poignantly captures his desperate mother kidding with her child in order to distract him while she tries to figure out how to feed him. However, he also hints at another dimension of his hunger when he recognizes that his mother is teasing him and becomes angry. Throughout *Black Boy*, Wright becomes enraged when he is not taken seriously, when his intellect, his integrity, or his dream to be a writer is belittled by anyone, white or black. In fact, interestingly, Wright's family members are frequently just as dismissive of his talents and abilities as the white world is, and his family members are certainly more persistent in their disdain. Young Richard is angry because his mother will not reason with him and explain to him why there is no food in the house. When she finally relents and helps Richard make the link between his father's absence and his hunger, Wright transfers his anger to his father, and "whenever [he] felt hunger [he] thought of him with a deep biological bitterness" (16). Young Richard resents the attempts of adults to shield him from harsh realities, for he is too perceptive to believe their evasions and falsehoods but too young to have direct access to all the information about his environment he craves.

Wright makes a more overt linkage between his physical hunger and his hunger for respect, for knowledge, for a life that would be richer both materially and intellectually later in the text when he "vowed that someday [he] would end this hunger of [his], this apartness, this eternal difference" (126). He shows the reader that he is starving physically, intellectually, and socially. Indeed, there is an important social dimension to his hunger. As we shall see, he also hungers to feel a sense of belonging to his fellow human beings, particularly to the black community, but a sense of belonging seems always to elude him.

Black Boy is permeated with references to hunger, both physical and spiritual. Wright painstakingly describes the meager diet of mush, greens, and lard he ate while living at his grandmother's house in Jackson, Mississippi. Just as he learned to associate hunger with his father's absence as a small child, he continues to lay blame for his hunger not only on the racial inequalities perpetuated by Jim Crow but on his family as well. One factor contributing to his hunger is his grandmother's staunch devotion to Seventh-Day Adventism, a religion that prohibits eating pork (the source of protein most widely available to poor southerners) as well as working on the religion's Sabbath, Saturday, which made it nearly impossible for Wright to get a part-time job to feed himself.

His grandmother's religion also contributed to Richard's intellectual hunger. She forbade him to read fiction, which she regarded unambiguously as "lies." Wright recalls that he had his first "total emotional response" when he defied his grandmother's rules and induced Ella, a young schoolteacher boarding at his grandmother's house, to tell him the story of "Bluebeard and his Seven Wives." Although Granny interrupted the story midstream, declaring it "devil stuff" and Ella an "evil gal," for Wright this encounter with a fictional world made a lasting impression and gave him a clue as to how he could hope to satisfy at least one dimension of his hunger. Again, he makes the comparison between intellectual and physical sustenance, declaring, "I had tasted what to me was life, and I would have more of it" (40).

In the hands of a less skilled writer, Wright's metaphor of hunger might appear heavy handed. In the hands of even a talented novelist, it might seem contrived. However, rooted as it is in the material world, in a deep and abiding physical hunger that was the result of nearly crippling poverty, his metaphor of being starved intellectually and socially is very effective. He shows his reader that the southern environment was so stifling that his desire to be free of it was as pressing as his need to have his minimum physical requirements met. Leaving the South and that environment was every bit as urgent to his survival as having enough food to eat.

Wright could not have conveyed his feelings of deprivation as effectively without comparing them to physical hunger. If he wrote, however earnestly, using literal language, something like, "I found the environment of the South intellectually stifling," he could not have conveyed the depths of his suffering. The metaphor of hunger allows the reader to refeel Wright's Jim Crow experience more effectively. Since he compares his intellectual and social longings to physical hunger, his readers, who have all experienced physical hunger to some degree, can draw on their own familiarity with that sensation in order to better understand his yearnings. Through Wright's use of the image of hunger to describe both his material and his spiritual state, the reader is reminded of the depths of Wright's deprivation. His very survival depended on finding a way to sate his hunger on many different levels.

Not only does Wright employ metaphor to describe his social reality effectively, but he also utilizes the literary device of irony to capture certain aspects of his felt experience of Jim Crow. Historians, of course, cannot employ metaphor or irony as effectively as can a literary artist. Although historians might use a metaphor briefly to make a point by means of comparison, they are unlikely to utilize a sustained metaphor like Wright's "hunger" throughout the text to impart meaning or for poetic effect. Since historical writing is typically received as a literal rather than a figurative kind of communication, the use of irony could be confusing and easily misinterpreted. As a literary artist, Wright has the tools of metaphor and irony at his disposal and can use them to convey meanings that historians and nonliterary memoirists cannot.

Relationships between whites and blacks in the segregated South were fraught with irony. Because of the code of conduct that whites expected black southerners to adhere to—what Wright refers to elsewhere as "the ethics of Jim Crow"—African Americans repeatedly found themselves in the position of being forced to say things that they did not literally mean. In many interactions between blacks and whites, when African Americans were forced to acquiesce to whatever the white person wanted to hear, other blacks served as a true audience who understood the real meaning behind these scripted encounters.

These kinds of layered communications have their roots, of course, in slavery. Slaves might sing spirituals that their masters would interpret as religious songs yearning for heaven and communion with God. However, the slaves themselves, the song's true audience, knew that references to geographies such as the river Jordan and the Promised Land hinted only secondarily at religious longings but were truly concerned with freedom from slavery and physical locations outside the South. Of course, this is southern irony in its most exaggerated form. Frequently it was much less complicated, as simple as a black person telling a white person "yes," to avoid repercussions, when she or he really meant "no."

Wright brilliantly inverts the device of irony to show how contrary adhering to the ethics of Jim Crow was to his character. He toys with his audience by not using irony in defiance of his readers' expectations. His protagonist, his younger self, is breathtakingly immune to the possibility of layered meanings. He attempts to communicate with the world around him on literal terms and is baffled when his earnest efforts are met with exasperation. One such interaction occurs when Richard receives his first job working for a white family as part-time domestic help. During his interview for the job he fails to perform as the social mores of his time dictated:

> "Do you want this job?" the woman asked.
>
> "Yes, ma'am," I said, afraid to trust my own judgment.
>
> "Now, boy, I want to ask you one question and I want you to tell me the truth," she said.
>
> "Yes, ma'am," I said, all attention.
>
> "Do you steal?" she asked me seriously.
>
> I burst into a laugh and then checked myself.
>
> "What's so damn funny about that?" she asked.
>
> "Lady, if I was a thief, I'd never tell anybody."
>
> "What do you mean?" she blazed with a red face.
>
> I had made a mistake during my first five minutes in the white world. I hung my head. (145)

Wright succinctly highlights the absurdity of the racial situation with this anecdote, which frighteningly reveals how little intelligence or sophistication this white woman had ascribed to her potential employee. This Jim Crow interaction comes as a shock to Wright, who is young, earnest, and eager to earn money to buy school clothes and books. Astonishingly, this encounter with the white woman reveals that he does not yet have the tools necessary to succeed in the southern caste system. He must learn to behave ironically in order to survive in this hostile environment.

Black Boy powerfully captures Wright's personal growth and his gradual understanding of his environment. He masterfully conveys various stages of his consciousness as he learns to negotiate the world around him. He does not enter the world with full-blown knowledge about how to survive in it. Instead he is to discover by trial and error what the world demands of him. It is common in African American fiction and memoirs and in histories of the African American experience to write about the moment a child becomes aware of American racism. For example, in "A Letter from Birmingham Jail," Martin Luther King Jr. recalls the agony of telling his daughter that "Funtown is closed to colored children, and see[ing] the depressing clouds of inferiority begin to form in her little mental sky."[4] The protagonist in Johnson's *Autobiography of an Ex-Colored Man* "discovered" he was black when a school official told him that he was different from his white classmates, giving him "a sword-thrust that day in school which was years in healing."[5] Wright, too, shows the reader how his consciousness as a black man was formed as he chronicles his growing awareness of the extent and the virulence of southern racism. However, he shows his reader that awareness comes to him in bits and pieces.

There is no huge, transformational moment when all becomes clear to Wright. Instead he evolves gradually. He painstakingly re-creates his thought processes for the benefit of his readers. In describing his personal evolution, he captures an important aspect of felt Jim Crow experience. His understanding of and sophistication in dealing with his environment change. A historian quoting from *Black Boy* might partly capture Wright's emotions and understanding of his social world at one particular moment, but as the full text of *Black Boy* reveals, Wright's partial revelations tend to grow and change. Wright biographers may be able to capture this change to some extent, but the complexity of his felt experience cannot be adequately conveyed in historical summary. One of the lessons Wright gradually learns is that he must figure out how to live ironically, to perpetually say one thing and mean another.

Wright's friend Griggs patiently advises him about how to get out of the way of white people, how to appear nonthreatening, how to keep a job, how to live in the South. Griggs has been able to master the art of surviving in the South, of appearing docile and contented while concealing a deep hatred for his oppressors. He tells Wright, "You know, Dick, you might think I'm an Uncle Tom, but I'm not. I hate these white people, hate 'em with all my heart. But I can't show it; if I did, they'd kill me" (185). At this point in his development, Wright is too naive and unskilled at southern irony to automatically constitute Griggs's true audience during interactions with whites. To make Wright understand, Griggs must painstakingly explain that he masks his true feelings in front of white people in order to survive.

Wright attempts to put Griggs's lessons into practice but soon finds it "utterly impossible . . . to calculate, to scheme, to act, to plot, all the time.

[He] would remember to dissemble for short periods, then [he] would forget and act straight and human again, not with the desire to harm anybody, but merely forgetting the artifice of race and class" (185). For Wright, to live "straight" and free of irony was a matter of pride. He wanted to look whites "straight in the face . . . to talk and act like a man" (200). By presenting himself as a naive but dignified teenager who cannot comprehend or remember to abide by the social code, he shows us how oppressive and how crippling to his personal identity Jim Crow was. Every word uttered or movement made had to be gauged for its impact on the whites around him. This kind of self-censorship did not come naturally to Wright, and by extension we can assume that other black southerners may have found it equally difficult to absorb the lessons of Jim Crow.

Ultimately, Wright learns how to behave in the South well enough that he manages to survive long enough to make his escape. After being dismissed from many jobs because he could not play by the Jim Crow rules, he eventually learns how to mask his true feelings. He also learns to adapt his personal ethics in another way when he decides to supplement his escape money by stealing. Theft violated his own sense of ethics just as much as shuffling, smiling, and pretending to acquiesce in the presence of his white employers. However, he eventually became desperate and calculating enough to temporarily violate his own moral code in order to escape. He could not live ironically, telling the white world what it wanted to hear and then taking comfort in the bosom of a black community that understood his true meanings. He had discovered that he was not suited for long-term survival in the South.

When he was finally ready to join the Great Migration northward, he showed how far he had evolved in learning the lessons of Jim Crow beyond his first encounter with the white woman who asked him if he was a thief. On his last day on the job, as he is taking his leave of the white men he worked for, he demonstrates that he has finally learned some of the lessons Griggs had attempted to teach him.

"How're you going to act up there?"
"Just like I act down here, sir."
"Would you speak to a white girl up there?"
"Oh, no, sir. I'll act just like I act here."
"Aw, no, you won't. You'll change. Niggers always change when they go north."

I wanted to tell him that I was going north precisely to change, but I did not.

"I'll be the same," I said, trying to indicate that I had no imagination whatever. (256)

In this passage, Wright demonstrates that he has at least partially mastered irony. He has learned to conceal his true feelings; however, he continues to have difficulty finding a true audience in the black community to understand his layered meanings. Wright directs anger and suspicion not only at the white world but also at the black community, including members of his own family. He reminds his readers that we cannot try to understand southern history in terms of race relations alone, and experiential understanding of Wright's experiences shows us that white racism was only one of many issues he grappled with as he came of age in Arkansas and Mississippi.

In one of the most controversial passages of *Black Boy*, a parenthetical aside in which the voice of the mature Wright blatantly interjects itself to comment on the experiences of his younger self, he remarks on "the absence of real kindness of Negroes." He continues his indictment, grimly noting "how unstable was our tenderness, how lacking in genuine passion we were, how void of great hope, how timid our joy, how bare our traditions, how hollow our memories" (37). Wright's descriptions of the black community in the text are surprisingly dismal. In fact, he appears almost as alienated from his family and his peers as he is from the white community. He blames white racists both for their own pathology and for what he viewed as the sorry psychological state of the black community. His intention in writing *Black Boy* was to "render a judgment on [his] environment."[6] In his estimation it was the brutal environment of Jim Crow that created the frailties he saw in black people, the absence of real kindness, bare traditions, timid joy, and so on. He believed that "the environment the South creates is too small to nourish human beings, especially Negro human beings."[7]

Wright's belief that racism crippled blacks psychologically even allowed him to feel a measure of pity for his father, who had deserted him as a child. Recalling a trip he made as an adult to visit his father in Mississippi, he writes: "I stood before him, poised, my mind aching as it embraced the simple nakedness of his life . . . how chained were his actions and emotions to the direct, animalistic impulses of his withering body. . . . From the white landowners above him there had not been handed to him a chance to learn the meaning of loyalty, of sentiment, of tradition. Joy was unknown to him. As a creature of the earth, he endured, hearty, whole, seemingly indestructible, with no regrets and no hope" (34).

As Wright describes it, his childhood, growing up among the children and grandchildren of slaves, was almost unremittingly bleak. He implies that it is only by sheer determination and a rich imagination that he has escaped his father's fate. He recounts poverty, hunger, abandonment by his father, a short stay in an orphanage, his mother's debilitating illness, and the lynching of an uncle all in very short order. His family life, instead of offering him comfort in the midst of external problems he has no control over, compounds his misery. His strict religious grandmother cannot understand her moody, imaginative grandson, and her disapproval sets the tone for how the entire family views Richard: as "brutal and desperate," unsaved and perhaps irredeemable (172). The sense of alienation that Wright describes during his childhood in the South follows him after he leaves Mississippi for Chicago. Upon arrival he claims, "In my life—though surrounded by many people—I had not had a single satisfying, sustained relationship with another human being" (261).

In a passage in the text similar in its poetic structure to his earlier catalog of rural pleasures, Wright recounts much of the African American folklore he heard as a child. He recites a list of twenty-five superstitions about what would happen if he broke a mirror, stepped over a broom, made fun of a crippled man, spit in his urine, and so on. This passage demonstrates that Wright was familiar with folk traditions, remedies, and wisdom. He even toys with the possibility that these superstitions could all be true: "Anything seemed possible, likely, feasible, because I wanted everything to be possible" (72). However, this brief description of folk wisdom quickly ends, and Wright never describes his integration into the community that spawned the wisdom he recites so earnestly. As Jay Mechling observes, "in *Black Boy* there is no sense of African-American folklore as a resource for living."[8]

Despite this feeling of alienation, Wright figures himself as a spokesperson for the black community. On the one hand, Wright is unabashed in his assertion that his life story is his alone. He recalls an epiphany he had at the age of twelve. He realized that he had "a sense of the world that was mine and mine alone . . . a conviction that the meaning of living came only when one was struggling to wring a meaning out of meaningless suffering" (100). Wright's conception of himself and his life is a solitary one.

He accepts his alienation from the southern white community, which rejects him, and also from the black community, which he believes misunderstands him. He is girded with his own feeling of exceptionality. In this regard, Wright's autobiography fits strongly within the Western tradition of life-writing as a celebration of uniqueness and one's accomplishments. However, Wright simultaneously figures himself as an exceptional individual on a solitary journey and as a racial spokesperson with a group identity.

Although *Black Boy: A Record of Childhood and Youth* was not Wright's original title for his memoir about his southern childhood, the title was his suggestion and was deliberately chosen after an ongoing discussion with his editor and the selection committee at the Book of the Month Club. His choice of the title indicates his desire to speak for a much larger group than just himself and his willingness to testify as a representative "black boy." He claimed, "One of the things that made me write is that I realize that I'm a very average Negro." This claim seems perplexing after his repeated disassociation from the black community of his youth. He recalls that his motivation in writing his memoir was that he "wanted to give, lend [his] tongue to the voiceless, Negro boys."[9] His willingness to speak for a group that he does not quite allow himself to belong to becomes a pronounced tension in the text, making Wright, despite his best intentions, appear as an ambivalent racial spokesperson.

As a self-described misfit, Wright marvels at the way that others are better able to negotiate life in the Jim Crow South than he is, yet he simultaneously claims to be a spokesperson for the collective experiences of black youth in the South. Herein lies one of *Black Boy*'s most compelling historical insights. When we read Wright's memoir with the goal of refeeling his experience, we see that an important dimension of his life was the tension between his assertion of both an individual and a group identity. We can imagine that this tension, which Wright began to experience as a child, only heightened as he grew in fame and stature as a writer and his connections with the southern black community of his youth weakened. Wright reveals the hardships of an African American writer struggling to find a way to combine allegiance to his craft, his self, and his feelings of duty to the community.

Wright views himself as set apart from the black community, affiliated but not an integral part even of his own family. Carla Cappetti has described Wright's role as creator of *Black Boy* as "three-fold . . . as informant, participant observer, and sociologist."[10] Wright does survey the cultural landscape of his childhood environment with a certain kind of detachment. After describing his classmates at a Seventh-Day Adventist school he attended as "will-less, their speech flat, their gestures vague, their personalities devoid of anger, hope, laughter, enthusiasm or despair, " he claims, "I was able to see them with an objectivity that was inconceivable to them" (104). He participates in the world, but he repeatedly inserts the suggestion that he is not of that world, that he is chronically misunderstood. His yearning to be somewhere else, doing something else, is so extreme that he never allows himself to become fully a part of that community. While attending church and surveying the congregation he recalls, "I longed to be among them, yet when with them I looked at them as if I were a million miles away" (151). It is almost as if Wright is playing the role of social scientist, living in a culture alien to him, observing what he saw, and biding his time until he can leave that environment.

In *Dust Tracks on a Road*, Hurston, too, owing to her training as an anthropologist and the participant-observer role all autobiographers fulfill, functions as a something of a social scientist. However, she does not maintain Wright's level of detachment from the black community, and her Jim Crow experience is a much different one as a result. For Hurston, African American culture thrives in spite of white oppression. For her, celebrating and practicing a rich, unique culture provides some insulation from, perhaps even compensation for, racial injustices. However, her position is complicated by an uneasy acknowledgment of the impact of white racism. Her depiction of life in the segregated South differs dramatically from Wright's depiction as a result.

Zora Neale Hurston, *Dust Tracks on a Road*

In contrast to *Black Boy*, Zora Neale Hurston's Jim Crow autobiography, *Dust Tracks on a Road*, is rooted in black folk culture. Hurston did not use either her creative writing or her autobiography to protest white racism, and she found the sense of community that Wright could not. As a result, her description of Jim Crow reality bears little resemblance to that depicted in *Black Boy*. Hurston's autobiography does not follow the traditional linkage in African American autobiography of freedom and geography. Hurston travels north to New York, where she attends Barnard College and participates in the Harlem Renaissance, but the South never loses its allure for her. She returns to it on numerous occasions, and biographical information about her reveals that, in a countermigration, she eventually returned to Florida, where she spent the rest of her life.

Unlike *Black Boy*, which has become heralded as the representative Jim Crow autobiography, *Dust Tracks on a Road* has not been widely embraced. *Dust Tracks* does not enjoy the same prominence as *Black Boy* in the footnotes of historical works about the Jim Crow era. Neither has it received the same kind of scrutiny as *Black Boy* from literary critics. Alice Walker views it as "the most unfortunate thing Zora ever wrote," an opinion shared by some other critics as well.[11] Hurston subverts her readers' expectations in a number of ways. *Dust Tracks* covers a larger period of the autobiographer's life than does *Black Boy*, which ends before Wright had achieved success as a writer. Hurston's autobiography begins with a description of her birth as described in her family folklore and ends at the time she wrote the autobiography. However, despite this fact, many, particularly those most interested in her fiction, have deemed *Dust Tracks* infuriatingly incomplete. Hurston devotes little space to describing her involvement with the Harlem Renaissance and not much more to the writing of her most prized books, *Jonah's Gourd Vine* and *Their Eyes Were Watching God*. In addition, the book concludes with a series of essays on topics such as friendship, religion, and love, which interrupt the book's already lopsided chronology. Most perplexing to many of her readers is her unwillingness to make race and racism central in her autobiographical account. It is in this regard that Hurston's vision of Jim Crow life differs most strikingly from Wright's.

Robert Hemenway has observed that *Dust Tracks* was "apparently written self-consciously with a white audience in mind."[12] Indeed, her editor, Bertram Lippincott, did ask Hurston to remove two chapters from the manuscript, one of which contained a strong indictment of American imperialism, which he felt would offend readers inspired to patriotic fervor as a result of the recent entry of the United States into World War II. Similarly, Alice Walker believes that Hurston's warm descriptions of white friends—and perhaps by extension, her refusal to comment on their racism—were "out of character" as well as "a result of dependency, a sign of her powerlessness, her inability to pay back her debts with anything but words." Walker refuses to believe Hurston's expressions of gratitude to white friends and patrons, claiming that the people Hurston thanked were individuals "one knows she could not have respected."[13] However, Hurston's complex views on the issue of race, which may indeed have been partially censored because of audience expectations and limited by societal strictures on free expression by a black woman, cannot be simply dismissed on this basis alone.

For Hurston, avoiding bitterness of any kind was a matter of pride. She proclaimed, "To me, bitterness is the under-arm odor of wishful weakness" (765). Anecdotal evidence about her willingness to overlook racial injustices, to silently conform to Jim Crow convention by uncomplainingly descending back staircases or sleeping in the servants' quarters when visiting prominent whites, is rife in Hurston biographies. Her most recent biographer, Valerie Boyd, recalls how Hurston would overlook rude treatment by waiters and the hostile stares of other customers when dining with her editor or others in New York City. Boyd speculates that Hurston reasoned that the "other customers' sullenness would not prevent Hurston from enjoying her free meal, unless she *allowed* it to have that effect."[14] Although unorthodox and politically suspect to people who believe racial injustice should be tackled head-on, by some measures her strategy proved to be surprisingly effective. Hurston became, for a time, a prominent African American woman of letters who was amazingly able to support herself as a writer and a researcher even during the lean years of the Great Depression.

Hurston was resentful of expectations forged in the black community that dictated that she should use her writing to fight racial oppression. When she sat down to write her first novel, *Jonah's Gourd Vine*, she was daunted not only by the vastness of the task but also by the series of expectations that she labored under as an African American writer. She recalled, "What I wanted to tell was a story about a man, and from what I had read and heard, Negroes were supposed to write about the Race Problem. I was and am thoroughly sick of the subject. My interest lies in what makes a man or a woman do such-and-so, regardless of his color" (713). Eudora Welty, a fellow southerner and a white woman, famously echoed Hurston's assertion that her craft should be separated from her politics in her 1965 essay "Must the Novelist Crusade?" In fact, Will Brantley convincingly argues that *Dust Tracks* has much more in common with Welty's memoir, *One Writer's Beginnings*, than it does with *Black Boy*.[15] In her autobiography, it is Hurston's expressed desire to recount her individual achievements and experiences as hers alone rather than as those of a representative black woman. To do so, she felt it necessary to separate herself from the "sobbing school of Negrohood" and to deny frequently the impact of racism on her life chances.[16]

A historian writing a history of the Jim Crow South would not likely choose to deemphasize southern racism—for political reasons as well as for reasons of historical accuracy. After all, state-sanctioned racism is the defining characteristic of the era. Hurston, in contrast, is not writing the history of an era but the history of her own life. Whether the decision to subvert racial issues represents calculation on her part, an accurate assessment of how she viewed the world, or a combination of these factors may be debatable. For whatever reasons, Hurston, by sheer force of will, pushed racism to the periphery of her life and her retelling of that life, placing herself on center stage in the process. Hurston's unusual decision gives her readers another insight into how Jim Crow could have been experienced. Segregation and other forms of discrimination may have impacted various individuals differently, owing not only to different life experiences but also to varied personal outlooks. While Hurston's choice to downplay racism may not have had any effect on the harsh, concrete realities of the Jim Crow social order, her worldview certainly affected the way she experienced her social reality.

Dust Tracks is peppered with disavowals of the significance of racism that have infuriated many of the text's readers. Even though Hurston was writing almost a quarter of a century before the civil rights legislation of the mid-1960s outlawed the most outward vestiges of racism, she startlingly claimed: "I do not share the gloomy thought that Negroes in American are doomed to be stomped out bodaciously, nor even shackled to the bottom of things. Of course some of them will be tromped out, and some will always be at the bottom, keeping company with other bottom folks. . . . We will go where the internal drive carries us like everybody else. It is up to the individual. If you haven't got it, you can't show it. If you have got it, you can't hide it. That is one of the strongest laws God ever made" (732–33). Hurston is not reflecting heady civil-rights-era optimism, writing as she was in an era when African Americans fighting against Nazis abroad were simultaneously waging a Double Victory battle against deeply held racism at home. Her belief that blacks could rise or fall according to individual attributes, even in the midst of a Jim Crow system designed to severely circumscribe their life chances, has startled many. Despite this avowal and other strong statements like it, elsewhere in *Dust Tracks* Hurston is less flippant in her belief in American meritocracy and grudgingly admits to racial inequalities. In one of the few passages in the book in which she alludes to segregation or to institutionalized racism, she expresses a deep ambivalence.

While she was a student at Howard University in 1919, she worked as a manicurist at a black-owned barbershop in Washington, D.C., that served only white customers. One day a black man came into the shop, sat in a barber's chair, and demanded to be served. The employees of the shop and the white customers banded together and physically threw the would-be customer out of the shop and onto the street with Zora's silent approval. Only later did she begin to reflect on what had taken place. She realized: "I was giving sanction to Jim Crow, which theoretically I was supposed to resist. But here were ten Negro barbers, three porters, and two manicurists all stirred up at the threat of our living through loss of patronage. . . . That was the first time it was called to my attention that self-interest rides over all sorts of lives" (679). She does think fleetingly that it might have been a "beautiful thing" if all the black workers had expressed solidarity with the would-be integrator. She finally avers that she does not know what the "ultimate right" was in that situation while simultaneously defending her first reaction by contending that there is something "fiendish and loathsome about a person who threatens to deprive you of your way of making a living" (680). This incident certainly reveals that Hurston was not in the vanguard of the direct resistance arm of the civil rights movement, but what else does this tell us about the way she experienced Jim Crow and navigated the racial realities of her day?

This anecdote seems designed to please neither a white nor a black audience. White readers opposed to integration might resent Hurston's acknowledgment that serving the black patron might have been a "beautiful thing." They might also note that Hurston's argument for not serving the man is not a defense of Jim Crow ethics. Instead, their refusal to serve him, thereby risking their livelihoods, was a result of the black employees' precarious economic position, which was itself an outgrowth of the Jim Crow system. Much of her black audience, of course, was appalled by the fact that she found it possible to justify segregation on any grounds. Such a mixed and unpopular position may indicate that Hurston was not playing to any particular audience and was instead conveying her own, unvarnished beliefs.

Her views on the Jim Crow system in the South and the racism in the North as expressed in *Dust Tracks* are complicated and sometimes contradictory. For example, in one passage she claims that she was "not conscious of [her] race no matter where [she might] go." However, in a passage later in the text she remarks offhandedly, "No Negro in America is apt to forget his race" (664, 721). So, which is it? Is she conscious of her status as a black woman or not? It would be hard to imagine that she did not confront racism daily while residing in the North. It would be absurd to defend the position that she did not think of her race while she was living or traveling in the South, where segregation was much more institutionalized than in the less outspokenly racist North. How could she avoid thinking about race when every move she made ranging from what railroad car she traveled on, to what water fountain she drank from, to where she could eat or sleep was dictated by her racial identification? Why would she go to great lengths to argue, even at the height of Jim Crow, that she had noticed "no curse in being black, no extra flavor in being white" when the entire Jim Crow system was ordered to ensure that such a situation existed? (731).

The answer to this question gives us an important insight into felt Jim Crow experience from Hurston's perspective and perhaps, by extension, from the perspective of other black southerners who shared Hurston's ambivalence. Hurston does not share Wright's singular focus to indict racism. Nor does she share the constancy of his anger and outrage at the Jim Crow system. Her reaction is more complex and just as logical a response to white racism as Wright's rage. Despite her protestations to the contrary, throughout *Dust Tracks* Hurston reveals that she is all too aware of the grim realities of racism, but she consistently resists letting the issue of racial injustice become central in her reminiscence.

Like so many other black autobiographers, Hurston records a moment of racial awakening when she left the all-black Florida town of Eatonville of her childhood to travel to Jacksonville, where she attended school. She recalled, "Jacksonville made me know that I was a little colored girl. Things were all about the town to point this out to me. Street cars and stores and then talk I heard around the school" (621). Passages such as this reveal undeniably that she was indeed painfully conscious of the grimmer aspects of the southern caste system. Why, then, elsewhere in the text does she proclaim that she is not conscious of her race? Why, after uttering these contradictory statements, doesn't she, a deliberate, reflective, artful memoirist, take the pains to reconcile them?

The contrary opinions that Hurston expresses are simultaneously contradictory and an accurate assessment of how she perceived Jim Crow. They reveal her understanding of the society she lived in both as she experienced it and as she wished it could be. Harold Bloom has labeled Hurston a "vitalist," who, like Walt Whitman, was full of exuberance and life.[17] She wanted to live in a world free of racism and sexism where she would be judged on her own considerable merits. She wanted this so much that sometimes she imagined it to be so. Other times racism was undeniably an obstacle, and she had to acknowledge it. Hurston's Jim Crow memoir is in part an honest reflection of what her life was like, in part a reflection of what she wished it had been. These kinds of competing visions are inextricably intertwined in all memories and in all histories.

Hurston gives her readers a clue about the way her memory functions in the often quoted first passage of her masterpiece, *Their Eyes Were Watching God*, when she declares, "Women forget all those things they don't want to remember, and remember everything they don't want to forget. The dream is the truth. Then they act and do things accordingly."[18] Elsewhere in *Dust Tracks* she acknowledges this same tension between dreams and reality, memory and willful forgetting. As a child she concocted a story about a neighbor who, she claimed, turned into an alligator at night. Even after the neighbor died, an ordinary and lonely death, she refused to abandon her story, claiming, "My phantasies were still fighting against the facts" (614). Perhaps the same could be said about her strong belief in meritocracy even in the midst of Jim Crow. Her ideals may not have meshed with the reality she'd been handed, but she clung to the ideals nonetheless.

An exchange with her father on the subject of Christmas presents reveals one of Hurston's Jim Crow coping mechanisms. As a child, she recalls being fascinated with the idea of traveling to the horizon. Unable to convince a friend to accompany her on the journey, she realized that she would have to go alone. However, she was reluctant to walk so far by herself. One year when her father asked her what she wanted for Christmas, she seized on the opportunity to secure a means of transportation for her trip, answering:

> "I want a fine black riding horse with white leather saddle and bridles," I told Papa happily.

"You what?" Papa gasped. "What dat you said?"

"I said, I want a black saddle horse, with . . ."

"A saddle horse?" Papa exploded. "It's a sin and a shame! Lemme tell you something right now, my young lady; you ain't white. Riding horse! Always trying to wear the big hat! I don't know how you got in this family nohow. You ain't like none of de rest of my young'uns." (584–85)

In this exchange, Hurston's father equates her grandiose Christmas wish with desiring to be white. In a footnote, Hurston interprets the expression "you ain't white" to mean "Don't be too ambitious. You are a Negro and they are not meant to have so much" (584). Her father, no doubt, expected her to request a doll or a new dress, and her grand desire struck him as presumptive and undeserved, the way white people assumed for themselves a disproportionate share of the South's material goods. His choice to scold her by making reference to the Jim Crow system shows that he was deeply aware of and impacted by injustices of this kind. It also reveals his fear that young Zora was expecting much more than her life as a black woman was likely to deliver. Elsewhere, Hurston's grandmother makes a similar observation when she tells her granddaughter, "They's gowine to lynch you, yet. . . . Youse too brazen to live long" (589). Hurston, however, responds to these warnings that she should learn to stay in her place by simply ignoring them. Although her father scolded her for even dreaming about owning a horse, Hurston simply invented one. She recalls, "Since Papa did not buy me a saddle horse, I made me one up. No one around me knew how often I rode my prancing horse, nor the things I saw in far places." When real life didn't suit her, she retreated to her imagination. She remembers, "I was driven inward. I lived an exciting life unseen" (585). These fantasies, this willful and imaginative ignoring of Jim Crow racism and inequalities, constituted Hurston's Jim Crow reality, the inside of her historical moment.

Dust Tracks is part dream, part reality, part wishful thinking, part cool assessment of the facts. Hurston does not feel compelled to reconcile these contradictions. In re-creating the chaos and the different ideas that she entertained at different times or sometimes simultaneously in varying degrees, Hurston allows her readers to more effectively refeel her Jim Crow experience. She gives her readers a hint about how to interpret her contradictions. Recalling the passionate words spoken in past love affairs, she claimed, "I was sincere for the moment in which I said the things. It is strictly a matter of time. . . . No two moments are any more alike than two snowflakes. . . . The great difficulty lies in trying to transpose last night's moment to a day that has no knowledge of it" (752). Felt experience is filled with ambivalence, with fantasies, and out-and-out contradictions. Pierre Walker has argued that *Dust Tracks* "portrays an individual persona that resists reduction to a coherent, consistent unity and instead portrays a person of many moods who is in tension with the world in which she moves."[19] Far from intending to criticize the text, Walker regards Hurston's autobiography as a brilliant description of a post-Enlightenment self, which is full of contradictions.

Sometimes Hurston alludes to her complexity of feelings about the racism of her day only indirectly. She, unlike Wright in his depiction of his younger self, is a master of irony. Hurston adeptly uses both irony and the black vernacular tradition. *Dust Tracks* is full of layered meanings, and the naive tone she assumes at times cannot be taken strictly at face value. However, because of Hurston's deep ambivalence, when she employs irony, she half believes the surface meaning even as she teases her true audience, ordering these readers to dig deeper. She straddles meanings and appears at least partially to embrace both levels of irony. Perhaps one level of irony, the surface meaning, can be said to represent what Hurston wishes were true, while the second layer reveals what she fears to be true.

As a child she formed an unlikely friendship with a "grey-haired white man" who used to take her fishing and give her advice, telling her, "Don't be a nigger. . . . Niggers lie and lie!" Despite the obvious racial subtext behind this peculiar friendship between a young black girl and a much older white man in Jim Crow Florida, Hurston claims that "the word Nigger used in this sense does not mean race. It means a weak, contemptible person of any race." In a deceptively naive tone she observes, "I knew without being told that he was not talking about my race when he advised me not to be a nigger. He was talking about class rather than race. He frequently gave money to Negro schools" (587).

Rather than directly questioning her friend's loaded word choice in dispensing advice or wondering why a discussion of social class, if that's indeed what occurred, should take place using such racialized terminology, Hurston claims on the surface to accept her companion's good intentions and to listen to his advice. However, her flippant observation that his motivations cannot be impugned because "he frequently gave money to Negro schools" adds another dimension to the interchange. Her defense of the white man is too easy, too ill considered, to be taken at face value. Hurston is alluding here to the absurd claim often made by unreflective whites that they are not racists because they, for example, "have a black friend." Hurston is telling her reader that she might have gone with the flow, gone fishing with the older white man, and listened to his advice, but she was not duped. She understood the power differential between them, the peculiarity of their friendship, and the dubious credentials many whites used to show that they were not racists even as they managed to thrive in a racist society. Whatever her friend's good intentions, they may have been accompanied by a condescension and a tokenism that Hurston shrewdly recognized even as a small child.

Similarly, in the last passage of the text as it originally appeared in 1942, Hurston brilliantly and ironically conveys a range of emotions about race and racism:

> I have no race prejudice of any kind. My kinfolks, and my "skinfolks"
> are dearly loved. My own circumference of everyday life is there. But I
> see their same virtues and vices everywhere I look. So I give you all my
> right hand of fellowship and love, and hope for the same from you. In my
> eyesight, you lose nothing by not looking just like me. I will remember
> you all in my good thoughts, and I ask you kindly to do the same thing
> for me. Not only just for me. You who play the zig-zag lightning of power
> over the world, with the grumbling thunder in your wake, think kindly of
> those who walk in the dust. And you who walk in humble places, think
> kindly too, of others. There has been no proof in the world so far that you
> would be less arrogant if you held the lever of power in your hands. Let
> us all be kissing-friends. Consider that with tolerable patience, we godly
> demons may breed a noble world in a few hundred generations or so.
> Maybe all of us who do not have the good fortune to meet or meet again,
> in this world, will meet at a barbecue. (769)

On one level she is preaching a gospel of racial reconciliation, urging whites who hold the "zig-zag lightning of power" to rule kindly and compassionately. She urges African Americans "who walk in humble places" to be patient, if not tolerant, of people in control, arguing that human nature is fundamentally the same and that, if power relations had been reversed, African Americans might not have been any less tyrannical than whites.

Daringly she assumes for a moment that this is the case, and she assures white Americans that they "lose nothing by not looking just like [her]" (769). By ironically assuming the posture of African American political and social dominance, she highlights the absurdity of white racial ideas while establishing herself as an authority figure, a standard worth emulating. Her hope for a future "noble world" is an ostensibly optimistic one that is marred by her seemingly offhanded timetable for racial reconciliation of "a few hundred generations or so," a time so distant that it exists only in her imagination and does not have a concrete foundation in the world as she knew it. Finally, she ends the passage with what on one level appears to be an appeal for interracial harmony, a metaphoric integrated barbecue perhaps in heaven. However, her choice of the term "godly demons," coupled with her reference to another world, causes Robert Hemenway to wonder whether, behind a mask of colloquial good humor and charm, "Zora is really telling her readers, 'I'll see you in Hell.' "[20]

Besides revealing a variety of contradictory and layered sentiments about race relations and the possibility of future interracial understanding, this passage also highlights another significant way in which her Jim Crow experiences differed from Wright's. Her declaration of her love for "kinfolks" and "skinfolks" reveals a deep sense of belonging to and love for the black community, which always eluded Wright. It is ironic that Wright, who fashioned himself a racial spokesperson, should find himself so alienated from the community he attempted to defend from white racism while Hurston, who actively resisted the role of spokesperson or representative black woman, felt so at home with other African Americans.

As many Hurston critics have noted, the tone of *Dust Tracks* is similar to that of a folktale. This stylistic choice roots this autobiography within the black vernacular tradition as well as within the literary tradition of autobiography. Hurston begins *Dust Tracks* by recounting the lore of the founding of the all-black town, Eatonville, where she grew up and then conveying the story of her birth as it was told to her. She claims, "Like the dead-seeming, cold rocks, I have memories within that came out of the material that went to make me. Time and place have had their say" (561). Lynn Domina observes that "Hurston does not confine the life she writes in her autobiography to the lifetime of her corporeal self but rather contextualizes—and extends—it temporally within the history of her community."[21] She is writing herself into the folklore of the community, picking her story up where the local oral histories and legends leave off. Like folktales, which are frequently less straightforward than they first appear, *Dust Tracks* contains layers of meaning as represented in Hurston's use of irony. *Dust Tracks* also contains fantastic elements common in some folktales. Hurston claims to have had a series of visions, "like clearcut stereopticon slides," that revealed to her what her future would hold (596). In addition to fashioning her own origins as something of a legend, Hurston recounts other folktales, stories, and songs throughout the text, interspersing them into her life narrative often without comment or transition as if they, too, are part of her life story. While folklore may not have been a resource for living in *Black Boy*, Hurston's autobiography is rooted in folk expression.

In chapter 5, "Figure and Fancy," Hurston lovingly describes "Joe Clark's store [which] was the heart and spring of the town" of Eatonville, Florida (599). Town residents sat on the porch swapping jokes and tall tales and fostering a good-natured sense of community that Hurston found irresistible. It was here that Hurston first heard about Brer Rabbit and Brer Fox. She learned about wordplay and innuendo. She felt a sense of community and warmth. She recalls lingering at the store, taking it all in until calls of "Zora-a-a! If you don't come here, you better!" would drive her reluctantly home (602). She recalls, "Life took on a bigger perimeter by expanding on these things. I picked up glints and gleams out of what I heard and stored it away to turn it to my own uses" (605).

These formative experiences shaped the kind of language she would speak, the kind of prose she would craft, and the trajectory her life would take. After working at a variety of odd jobs, traveling across the South as a lady's maid to a vaudeville performer, attending school at Morgan College and at Howard, Hurston found herself at Barnard College studying with renowned anthropologist Franz Boas. After studying with Boas, Hurston embarked on what was to be her parallel vocation alongside her writing, that of anthropologist. Her first mission to the South to collect folktales was her least successful, she recalls: "The glamour of Barnard College was still upon me. I dwelt in marble halls. I knew where the material was all right. But, I went about asking, in carefully accented Barnardese, 'Pardon me, but do you know any folk tales or folk songs?' The men and women who had whole treasuries of material just seeping through their pores, looked at me and shook their heads" (687). Hurston quickly remedied the situation by returning to her folk roots. She became the truest kind of participant observer, traveling throughout the South, living among black communities, collecting (and probably dispensing) vast amounts of folklore and folk wisdom.

As Henry Louis Gates Jr. observes, throughout *Dust Tracks* Hurston straddles "the linguistic rituals of the dominant culture and those of the black vernacular tradition."[22] Unlike Wright, who writes in standard English throughout *Black Boy*, Hurston interjects her prose, her "Barnardese" as she would have it, with folk expressions. She moves easily between them. She inserts sly colloquialisms throughout, telling her reader, for example, at one point that she had "friended with Big Sweet" (696). Playing the role of front-porch storyteller, she anthropomorphizes the trees in her yard as a child, writing, "There was another tree that used to creep up close to the house around sundown and threaten me. It used to put on a skull-head with a crown on it every day at sundown and make motions at me" (605). The musicality of her language choices, the indirection, the extended fantasies (such as her detailed description of the adventures of Miss Corn-Cob and Mr. Sweet Smell—a corn husk and a bar of soap that she played with as a child) all figure her as a storyteller in the tradition of Joe Clark's porch and show how rooted she was in that community. However, when she sits down to write *Dust Tracks*, she is also an outsider, writing about a world that she is no longer completely a part of.

Will Brantley observes, "Throughout *Dust Tracks* . . . Hurston identifies the presence of a reader whose range of cultural experience is clearly not her own."[23] She includes footnotes that interpret folk expressions for readers unfamiliar with them. Sometimes she inserts herself as an editorial presence when conveying folktales, remarking, for example, what "the usual rejoinder was" to a certain exchange (601). She also occasionally uses quotation marks to indicate words outside standard English like "ruint" or "bigged" (600). Not only does Hurston use these techniques to translate the world of Joe Clarke's front porch for a readership unfamiliar with it, but her wide-ranging cultural fluency and her ability to effortlessly shift back and forth reveal the complexity of Hurston's recollections of her Jim Crow experience.

Much like Wright, Hurston felt conflicted between her conceptions of herself as a unique individual and as group member. Robert Hemenway observes that "Zora seems to be both an advocate for the universal, demonstrating that this black woman does not look at the world in racial terms,

and a celebrant of a unique upbringing in an all-black village."[24] It is striking that both Hurston and Wright felt torn between their individual selves
and their group identities. It is likely that other African American southerners felt similarly conflicted. Both alternatively fought against and embraced
the idea that black autobiographers spoke not only for themselves but also
for the community. However, despite this similarity, the way each describes
his or her community of origin remains strikingly different.

Both Wright's and Hurston's Jim Crow memories are written from another place, geographically, educationally, and emotionally. Wright wrote
about growing up in Mississippi while living in New York City, having escaped from the South he detested and having managed not only to educate
himself but also to become a famous writer. Looking at his past from that
vantage point, he felt only bitterness. Hurston wrote from a similarly distant place. Geographically, she wrote *Dust Tracks* in the California home of
her wealthy friend Katharine Edson Mershon. She was at that point college
educated, a published writer, and a well-traveled anthropologist. However,
when she surveyed her Jim Crow experience, she did so with a much wider
range of emotions than did Wright.

Whereas Wright wrote about a distant world to which he did not plan to
return, Hurston wrote about a southern community she loved deeply and
still felt very much a part of. They recount some similar experiences of poverty, family difficulties, and the overpowering desire to get an education.
However, Hurston writes about many experiences Wright does not, such as
the childhood games she played, a crush she had on a teacher, and school
parties. Wright's indictment of his environment was so pervasive that it
precluded many positive recollections. Hurston, in contrast, recalled moments of joy in her childhood and a fondness for her community of origin.
Her depiction of black community life in the Jim Crow South is characterized by joy, storytelling, social gatherings, a world that thrived in spite of
racism. Wright, however, described a community pathologically damaged
by Jim Crow.

Despite the differences in their attempts to narrate history, both Wright
and Hurston wrote from the depths of the institutionalized racism of Jim
Crow. They both came of age decades before the civil rights movement
offered a full-blown challenge to the region's racial mores. In contrast,
Henry Louis Gates Jr. was born in 1950 and grew up during the years of the
struggle for black political and social equality. Throughout his childhood,

Gates's experiences were shaped by aspects of both the segregated South and the new racial order that southerners, white and black, were struggling to define.

Henry Louis Gates Jr., *Colored People*

Gates straddled not only a chronological borderland but also a geographical one. He was born in Piedmont, West Virginia, which is much closer to Pittsburgh than to Memphis, the capital of the Mississippi Delta region where Wright spent his formative years. Even at the height of Jim Crow, the social landscape of Gates's childhood did not have the psychological power that Mississippi held on the African American imagination; nor were the racial boundaries as deeply entrenched in rural West Virginia as they were in the Deep South.

The black residents of Piedmont numbered 351 out of 22,000 at the time of Gates's birth. They lived in a largely segregated social world, and until 1955, when the local school system "desegregated without a peep," they attended separate schools.[25] Despite the relatively smooth transition into integrated education that Gates describes, the vestiges of Jim Crow were everywhere, particularly in the areas of job and housing discrimination. Gates recalls that "almost all the colored people in Piedmont worked at the paper mill and made the same money, because they all worked at the same job, on the same platform" (8). Not only were blacks in Piedmont limited occupationally, but they also faced restrictions in the realm of housing, regardless of their income. Gates offhandedly tells his readers, "Colored people were hindered from owning property in Piedmont throughout the years of my childhood, our houses were always rented" (202).

Thus, it is clear that the general racial philosophy, the tendency to push blacks to the margins and to circumscribe their life chances, was the same in Piedmont as it was elsewhere in the South. The difference between the town of Gates's childhood and that of Wright's was in the degree of the racism and in the proportion of blacks to whites rather than in terms of the general intentions of the community toward its black inhabitants. Gates actually lived to see some of the changes instituted in his community that Wright and Hurston could only fantasize about, but in the aftermath of desegregation, Gates felt nostalgic for the separate "colored" world that existed prior to integration. Although Hurston likely could have identified with Gates's longing for the close-knit community of his childhood, Wright probably would have found Gates's sentimentality in this regard incomprehensible.

Gates's felt experience of Jim Crow gives us important historical insights partially because he recollects a slightly different historical moment and a somewhat different geographical space than do Wright and Hurston. However, his recollections are also historically intriguing because Gates is self-consciously the heir of Wright, the heir of Hurston, the heir of other black intellectuals who came of age before him. When he sat down to write *Colored People*, he did so having already read other memoirs of the time period, already familiar with the arduous task of being a representative black man, and hearing the voices of those who came before him in his ear. Interpreting Gates's memoir as a historical source presents a unique set of challenges for this very reason.

By the time *Colored People* appeared in 1994, Gates was solidly established as one of the most prominent black intellectuals in the country and a literary critic to boot. While writing his memoir, Gates had to have been mindful not only of the memoirist's goal of capturing a particular historical moment but also of the onerous task of writing his way into the literary tradition he had devoted his life to studying. Gates's status as a public intellectual has made many people view his reminiscence with a higher degree of suspicion than has been applied to memoirs written by less prominent individuals. Did he self-consciously write a memoir that would fit into the parameters of his own literary criticism? Undoubtedly this is almost certainly in part true. However, we are naive if we assume that other autobiographers are not, in their own fashion, doing the same thing—writing not only about what actually happened but also about what they thought happened, what they wished had happened, or what they think should have happened.

Because of Gates's gender, it is tempting to try to see *Colored People* as a successor to *Black Boy*. Because Wright's voice was so powerful and, for many, so definitive, black male writers ever since have had to contend with the shadow he cast with his groundbreaking novel *Native Son* (1940) as well as by his enormously influential autobiography. Other writers have had to engage with Wright either by seeing themselves as his heirs or by fighting against the impression he left on the social and historical landscape, finding ways to complicate and challenge Wright's vision. Some, like Ralph Ellison and James Baldwin, grappled with Wright's legacy overtly and publicly. However, this is not the case for Gates, who does not seem to view himself as a competitor of Wright as much as a protégé of Hurston. The cast of colorful folk characters that Gates tries to recapture in his text are people Hurston would have recognized and liked. Although Gates could identify with some of Wright's anger in the face of southern injustice, his Jim Crow coping mechanisms have much more in common with those employed by Hurston.

When mining a memoir for historical insights into felt experience, one of the greatest challenges comes in trying to decipher the voice, to discern whether the autobiographical narrator's voice rings true. Many reviewers of *Colored People* have struggled with this very question. For example, writing in *The Nation*, Jill Nelson accuses Gates of presenting a version of his "boyhood and early life that seems somehow sanitized."[26] As students of history reading autobiography, we often encounter passages that defy our expectations. When this occurs, we must measure our own impressions against the historical record and then ask ourselves what stories of our own are we bringing to our reading of the text. Does the voice sound inauthentic merely because it is not saying what we wish it to say or not using the stylistic techniques we are predisposed to favor? Alternately, are we ascribing truth value to an account merely because it matches and does not challenge our preconceptions? In the case of Gates, we must ask ourselves whether we are bringing our own ideas about a grown-up Harvard academician and using that image to judge Gates's attempt to reconstruct a younger self who had not yet set foot in Harvard Yard.

In the case of *Colored People*, the question of autobiographical voice is a particularly challenging one, one made even more complicated by Gates's own admission that he wrote the book "in [his] father's voice—in a black vernacular one."[27] His decision to write autobiography in a voice other than his own sounds potentially self-defeating and might explain some of the criticisms *Colored People* received. However, by writing in his father's voice, what Gates is trying to do is to recapture his own childhood voice, whose intonations must have had much in common with those of his father. He tells his daughters that his memoir was written from the "point of view of the boy [he] was" (xvi).

Indeed, Gates's memoir is infused with colorful folkisms—sometimes these phrases are interjected seamlessly into the text, becoming an organic part of Gates's own language. Other times they are ensconced in quotation marks, ensuring a vast distance between contemporary, Ivy League Gates and the Piedmont of his childhood. Using quotations, he captures the language of the African American community in Piedmont by referring, for example, to the mixed reception given "Dr. King and dem" and later to the sexual misadventures in the tiny town of Piedmont as "sneakin' and creepin'" (25, 57). However, at other times, sans distinguishing punctuation, he envelopes the language, wrapping it up as his own and limiting the distance between himself and these expressions. Later on, he refers—in his own voice—to sexual escapades as doing the "nacky-nacky" and also vividly describes how, at a picnic sponsored by the paper mill, "Inez Jones, with George Mason's white handkerchief dangling between her legs, did the dirty dog to end all dirty dogs" (57, 216).

Gates's decision to alternately record—as a detached participant observer—the linguistic patterns and the sensibilities of his community and then, abruptly, employ these devices and embrace these aesthetics himself has been discomfiting to many of his critics. Indeed, for any reader of *Colored People*, it is initially difficult to bridge the gap between the image of the polished Gates, the academic powerhouse, and the obscure Gates, the child in Piedmont whom he is attempting to rescue from historical oblivion. However, in attempting to subvert his contemporary identity and to foreground his younger self, Gates's challenge is not unique. One is reminded of Zora Neale Hurston's sometimes troubled attempts to navigate between the folk expressions of her childhood and the "Barnardese" she acquired during her college education.

Gates attempts to reconstruct the segregated world of his childhood, reporting on issues as diverse as the social events that folks in Piedmont enjoyed, their taste in TV shows, the elaborate lengths many went through to style and straighten their hair, and their religious beliefs and liturgical tastes. However, the mature narrator inevitably lurks on the edges of these recollections, sometimes overtly. For example, Gates recalls an exchange he had with his young daughter Maggie about her paternal grandmother. While driving in the car with his daughter, Gates recalled how magnificent and elegant his mother had been as a younger woman. Maggie, having met her grandmother only after she had aged and had been largely swallowed by a crippling depression, is somewhat dubious, telling her father, "Too bad she was never like that when *I* knew her." Startled, Gates replies, in his best

"Harvardese," "That was a terribly rude thing to say!" (20, 30). His prim, schoolboy response reveals the large distance he has traversed, particularly when compared with the language employed by Gates's father, which, as recorded by Gates, is full of wit, sarcasm, and wordplay. One gets the sense that Daddy Gates would have responded to Maggie's impertinence more memorably and colorfully.

However, Gates is left with no choice but to attempt this delicate negotiation between his older self and his younger self, between the education he acquired in his daily life in Piedmont and that afforded him in the academy. He, like all chroniclers of the past, must juggle history and memory and balance his contemporary self with his attempts to reconstruct a past self and a disappeared world. By lingering prominently in the margins of his reminiscence, Gates is upfront with this dilemma. If he appears to some of his readers to be detached from his Piedmont self, it is because it cannot be otherwise. However, must the problematic nature of historical reconstruction necessarily invalidate his entire characterization of his past?

Gates gives his readers insights into the process of leaving a warm, segregated black community for a wider, integrated world. He makes this transition in stages, by attending first the newly integrated local primary and secondary schools in Piedmont and later Yale University. It is a gradual process, which we see glimpses of, as Gates begins to toy with ideas and political viewpoints foreign to his relatives. He begins to sense a growing intellectual distance between himself and his kin, which is revealed in a fishing trip he took with his Uncle Nemo and his friend Mr. Bump while on a visit home from college. His Uncle Nemo remarked, definitively, that it is impossible to be both a Christian and a communist. Gates, the college student, promptly informed him that all the inhabitants of Poland were both, that these two characteristics were not mutually exclusive. Immediately he regretted his boldness, his attempt to impose his book learning on these older men. He remembers, "I never lied to Uncle Jim [Nemo] or Mr. Bump, but I did try to put things in such a way that they could climb inside what I had said" (164). It is clear that intellectually Gates begins to feel like he has outgrown many of his relatives. Although readers of *Colored People* might wince at Gates's condescension, he exemplifies a central dilemma faced by all narrators of history. Historians must simultaneously inhabit the rarefied realm of academia even as they try to capture the intricacies of the world outside those hallowed halls. How does one try to make sure that Nemo and Bump's voices become part of the historical record without changing them or qualifying them? Gates's critique of their worldview is one that is no doubt shared by many of his readers who might be charmed or bemused by Nemo and Bump but who would never substitute Piedmont folk wisdom for the worldview offered by higher education.

Although in this scene we do see Gates directly confronting his bitter-sweet journey away from home, in much of *Colored People* he presents mere vignettes. He paints vivid linguistic portraits of his loved ones without commenting on them. It is this aspect of the memoir that critics have found the most problematic. Gerald Early has argued that Gates is trapped in "rhetorical and cultural conventions that never truly examine anything, not least the assumptions upon which they are built. They certainly fail to examine Gates' main assumption, which is that personal, surface descriptions of picturesque, cultural rituals are explanations of the nature of those rituals and the culture that they memorialize."[28] Similarly, Elaine Ognibene claims that "the reader is left searching for missing pieces that would provide a whole story."[29]

Among other things, these reviewers long for Gates to explicitly reflect more on his relationship with his father, his sexual attraction for white women, and what the black cultural expression (often in the form of food, music, dance, and worship) that he describes so movingly *means*.[30] Indeed, *Colored People* offers much more of a snapshot—one no doubt retouched and placed sentimentally in a carefully selected frame—than a critique. Gates writes less as a scholar and more as a son, a cousin, a friend. Because his readers know him best as a literary critic, many seem surprised that he is no less immune to nostalgia about his childhood than are many of the rest of us. However, perhaps in not assuming a critical distance, in narrating without explicating, Gates is doing us a favor. Is it not possible that he is indeed capturing, to the best of his literary ability, his felt experience of growing up in the twilight of segregation? If so, he certainly would not be the first person to accept the parameters of his childhood world uncritically.

Perhaps readers of *Colored People* struggle with the text not only because Gates does not survey his childhood from scholarly heights but also because he does not tell the story of segregation that has become the historical consensus. In the fallout after the end of the civil rights movement, many black activists began to critique the ethics of or desirability of integration, sharing James Baldwin's skepticism about the merits of gaining entry into a "burning house" in the first place.[31] However, in general, a belief in the desirability of integration still forms the backbone of the predominant historical narrative. The *Brown* decision, which desegregated schools, and the Civil Rights Act of 1964, which outlawed discrimination in public accommodations, have been rightfully hailed as grand, transformational accomplishments. These developments fit neatly into the narrative of American progress, which still retains much of its power, certainly in the public imagination.

Although many scholars and activists have highlighted the limitations of judicial and legislative attempts to end racism by integrating schools and facilities, by and large the metanarrative of America is one that extols integration above all, that has enshrined King's dream as superior to all others. Indeed, Gates is a shining testament to the power that increased access has had on the lives of many people of color. Gates, no doubt, would be the first to acknowledge this, and his life story fits nicely into the cherished American myth of color blindness.

However, despite the gains he made as a result of the dismantling of Jim Crow, Gates's transition into the new social order was accompanied by a profound sense of loss, an emotion not accounted for in the formulaic narrative of American progress. Sanford Pinsker notes that what sets *Colored People* apart from many other memoirs about African American childhood is "a sense of nostalgia for, rather than yearning to escape from, the cultural conditions of his childhood."[32] Pinsker claims that part of what he labels as "nostalgia" stems from the fact that "Gates is comfortable with his blackness in ways that most black memoirists are not."[33] This claim is a minefield, and most readers, no doubt, would take issue with this ill-defined and blanket assertion that Gates is somehow more comfortable with "blackness" than black memoirists who had different historical experiences. For example, Early argues that Gates's notions of blackness are "cliché-ridden," that his account is somehow affected, that "the writer's blackness is being too much acted out for his public."[34] Whatever the analysis, it is clear that many readers find Gates's portrayal of what it was like to be black somehow at odds with their expectations, somehow out of sync with the way other black memoirists have characterized their understanding of race.

In this respect, *Colored People* is much like Hurston's *Dust Tracks on a Road*. Gates, quite simply, tells a different story than the one many of his readers expected to hear. Being no stranger to the black literary tradition,

Gates is likely aware of his readers' expectations and deliberately chooses not to place himself in the black protest tradition as exemplified by Richard Wright and James Baldwin. Race relations are central in nearly every historical work about African American southerners in the twentieth century, and certainly this is the case in representative autobiographies like *Black Boy* or Maya Angelou's *I Know Why the Caged Bird Sings*. Gates's autobiography bears the strong imprint of race consciousness and race pride, but it is lacking either in analysis of southern racism or in the indictment of it that is so common in other works chronicling the same time period.

When reading any memoir as historical source material, we must be careful not to conflate the story we think we are going to hear or the story we would like to hear with an authentic voice documenting felt experience of Jim Crow. After all, what evidence do we have that Gates's recollections, his voice, is skewed to a higher degree than is the case with any other historical witness? The people, places, and events that he describes in the text are externally verifiable. They are real. However, their meaning, their significance, rests in Gates's own perceptions and misperceptions of this historical moment. He must cater to his own recollections, his own experiences— which were constitutive of his historical moment—rather than to what a more removed and analytical reader is expecting to hear.

Gates's youthful attempts to deal with southern racism bear something in common with both Wright's and Hurton's approaches. Like Wright, he is forthcoming with evidence of racial inequalities. In addition to the housing and job discrimination that institutionalized racial differences in Piedmont, Gates gives us insights into instances of racial prejudice that happened on a more individualized level. We learn, for example, that Gates's brother was denied an academic prize on the basis of race, that his mother worked as a maid for a white woman who was unkind to her, and that Gates himself was discriminated against for dating a white woman. However, for the most part, these revelations are made rather offhandedly. The reader is not lambasted with rage or with an indictment of the system like we see in *Black Boy*. Although Gates is more willing to acknowledge racism than Hurston, his approach to dealing with its effects is much closer to hers than to Wright's.

In the preface to *Colored People*, written in the form of a letter to his two daughters, Gates writes, "I rebel at the notion that I can't be part of other groups, that I can't construct identities through elective affinity, that race must be the important thing about me. . . . I want to be black, to know black, to luxuriate in whatever I might be calling blackness at any particular time—but to do so in order to come out the other side, to experience a humanity that is neither colorless nor reducible to color" (xv). Like Hurston, Gates longs to emphasize the positive attributes he associates with blackness—the rich cultural tradition and the sense of belonging he felt as a member of a small and close-knit community. He does so, like Hurston, at the expense of minimizing the impact and the cruelty of racial discrimination. Gates realizes, ironically, that without segregation, without institutionalized racism, the "sepia toned" world of his childhood would not have existed.[35] Rejection by the white world made the black community much tighter and in fact created, by means of that exclusion, the parameters of the group of "colored people." Gates does not deny that he grew up in a racist environment or that white supremacy worked to the detriment of him and his family in some instances, but this fact was not the most important one to his younger self.

Perhaps what stood out to young Gates (as well as to the older Gates trying to recapture his younger self) was the warmth of his family life and not the injustices of the greater world they inhabited. Perhaps his family successfully shielded him from much of life's harshness. Given that he came of age at the tail end of Jim Crow, his adult world was a different one than that of his parents. The limitations imposed by Jim Crow were not as apparent to him as they were to Richard Wright. Interestingly, as nostalgic as Gates seems for the segregated Piedmont of his childhood, in his assessment integration was even more difficult and the sense of loss even more profound for the older members of his family. He argues that, for many older residents of Piedmont, "integration was experienced as a loss. The warmth and nurturance of the womblike colored world was slowly and inevitably disappearing" (184).

For Gates, integration was accompanied by both a sense of opportunity and a sense of loss. He reveled in the nurturing black community of his childhood even as he took full advantage of all the opportunities offered to him by the changing world. He enjoyed living in his childhood universe, but he also managed to escape the limitations posed by life in the rural South. By any measure, Gates became remarkably successful in his chosen field. Is it any wonder, then, as he looks back on his childhood, that he does so fondly, describing a black community that existed because of and in spite of discrimination but was not defined by it? He flirts with questions about identity, about blackness, about representation throughout the text, but he deliberately does not let these weighty issues sully his positive memories. His survival strategy was to deny the possibility of race as a hindrance, much like Hurston. He proudly embraces his race and becomes something of a cultural nationalist, but he refuses to let race define him or limit him— not even in the realm of his recollections.

Not only does Gates emphasize race pride at the expense of racism in the minds of many of his critics, but he also complicates many other classic narratives that have been enshrined in our understanding of the black experience. Although *Colored People* recounts the 1950s and 1960s, it is not a memoir about the civil rights movement. In fact, we catch only glimpses of the monumental struggle, which impacted Gates's life directly after the local schools were integrated but otherwise existed as a "spectator sport" viewed on television (27). Gates and his family watched the forces of massive resistance battle with the would-be integrators at places like Little Rock's Central High School as if they were viewing "a war being fought overseas" (27). In fact, members of the local community did not necessarily see the participants in the movement as heroes. Daddy Gates was "jaundiced about the civil rights movement, and especially the Reverend Martin Luther King, Jr. He'd say all of his names to drag out the scorn" (26). As Gates himself became somewhat radicalized as a result of his growing exposure to new ideas, he grew a tentative Afro, which was viewed with scorn by his relatives on his mother's side who called him "Malcolm" and "Stokely" with the "purest derision" (185).

His strategy for negotiating between his growing radicalism and his family's scorn, as well as between the necessary acknowledgment that racism limited the life chances of many blacks and the fact that he managed to thrive in spite of it, was to respond with irony. Like Hurston, Gates uses irony to describe race relations in Piedmont. He tells us:

All things considered, white and colored Piedmont got along pretty well in those years, the fifties and early sixties. At least as long as colored people didn't try to sit down in the Cut-Rate or at the Rendezvous Bar, or eat pizza at Eddie's, or buy property, or move into the white neighborhoods, or dance with, date or dilate upon white people. Not to mention try to get a job in the craft unions at the paper mill. Or have to get a drink at the white VFW, or join the white American Legion, or get loans at the bank, or just generally get out of line. Other than that, colored and white got along pretty well. (27–28)

This passage succinctly encapsulates Gates's felt experience of Jim Crow. The excerpt is laden with sarcasm as Gates makes a damning case establishing racial exclusion and then flippantly remarks, despite the overwhelming and ironic list of evidence to the contrary, that race relations were harmonious. However, there is also a layer of truth to his assertion that "colored and white got along pretty well." When Gates was a child, the white world was vague to him. Racial realities were abstract, and he initially was not sophisticated enough to attribute any of the difficult aspects of his life to the grim realities of the southern caste system. For the most part, whites were "only shadowy presences in our world," stock characters who came into focus only to serve specific functions and then left the community as quickly as they came: "Mr. Mail Man, Mr. Insurance Man, Mr. White-and-Chocolate Milk Man, Mr. Landlord Man" (11). While the presence of a vague, external white world was terrifying and oppressive to Wright, this was not the case for Gates, no doubt because of a number of factors including, but not limited to, geography, chronology, socioeconomic status, and the temperament of each. Gates's Jim Crow experience cannot be labeled definitive any more than Wright's, but it is certainly one important part of a larger, multiperspectival whole.

Gates chooses not to dwell on anger and injustice, hitting his readers with a dose of searing irony only to resume quickly his account of his love affair with the black community in Piedmont. We are invited to visualize charming scene after domestic scene, such as Gates playing with paper dolls in the family kitchen while his mother sewed. However, Jill Nelson is critical of Gates's tendency not to hit his readers harder with more introspection and analysis, comparing him to a "novice striptease dancer (or an aging pro) . . . [who] shyly refuses to take it all off, take it all off."[36] Perhaps, as a Jim Crow survival strategy, Gates could not allow himself to truly absorb the injustices that he encountered on a daily basis. Perhaps his tendency to minimize the cruelty in life and to concentrate on the cozy scene in the family kitchen explains his ability to thrive beyond Piedmont, to make his way into the upper echelons of the white-dominated academy. Instead of faulting Gates for not providing us with a more searing meditation on the impact of racism, perhaps we should read *Colored People* as something of a survival manual, as a way to thrive in spite of segregation, to beat the odds. If this was Gates's strategy for surviving Jim Crow, might not other black southerners have done the same thing?

One of Gates's most compelling contributions to our understanding of Jim Crow and our attempts to refeel a past moment comes in his ability to capture his sense impressions of a vanished world. In his provocative work *How Race Is Made: Slavery, Segregation, and the Senses*, Mark M. Smith argues that when historians talk about race, correctly, as a social construction they "still understand that construction as a largely visual enterprise."[37] However, Smith suggests that there is no "compelling reason for historians to fixate on what was seen rather than heard, smelled, tasted, and touched."[38] Smith makes a convincing case for how whites have historically designated blacks as "other," using a range of sensory impressions beyond skin color to justify making this distinction. For their part, blacks used rigorous critiques to challenge and disarm these spurious constructions of blackness, arguing, for example, against the stereotype that black people smelled bad by essentially agreeing with their detractors. According to Smith, blacks argued, "We smell; but if you worked as hard as we do in the conditions we do, you would smell, too."[39]

Gates is aware of this stereotype in particular and recalls community attempts to dispel this myth: "One thing we always did was smell good, partly because we liked scents, but partly because white people said we smelled bad *naturally*, like we had some sort of odor gene" (35). However, even as Gates describes black attempts to challenge white olfactory stereotypes about blackness, he confesses that the black community, too, held racialized ideas about white smells, believing, for example, that white people smelled like dogs when they got wet. Gates, the young empiricist, challenged this notion at the newly integrated swimming pool but was ultimately unsuccessful in convincing his mother that her sensory stereotypes about whiteness were no more true than white ideas about blackness (36).

Most of the time, however, Gates does not offer a critique of multiple-sensory constructions of race as much as try to capture his own sense impressions of what it meant to be "colored people." Gates, the intellectual, would almost certainly rebel against essentialist notions of racial difference, but it is clear that Gates's historical memory of his childhood world is laden with sense memories. Frequently he uses his senses to help define his community in opposition to a white world that looked, smelled, felt, and tasted much different.

As Gates recalls his childhood, some of the most evocative passages recall the way his childhood tasted, and he uses taste to establish racial differences between the white and black communities. Speaking for all of black Piedmont, he flippantly remarks, "White people can't cook; everybody knew that" (38). In poetic passage after poetic passage, he movingly describes the food he ate as a child, recounting the general understanding about how foods should be prepared. We learn, for example, that white food is bland and vegetables are undercooked (38–39). Furthermore, "white people," according to Mama Gates, were "*dirty*: They tasted right out of pots on the stove. Only some kind of animal, or the lowest kind of trash, would ever taste out of a pot on the stove" (35). To black residents of Piedmont, being a "colored" person meant having, in a sense, superior taste. They experienced racial differences through their senses, and in the opinion of Gates's family, black people came out ahead, enjoying, among other things, "fried chicken everywhere, and one of Nemo's wild turkeys, the kind where the skin stays crisp, especially around the darkest meat. Sweet pickles, olives, and celery on the side, of course" (169). Sensitive readers utilizing Gates's memoir as a historical tool are able to refeel, using all their senses, Gates's historical moment thanks to skillful literary and sensory descriptions.

Although Gates's accomplishments are the epitome of the promises of those civil rights activists who advocated integration, sometimes even believing in the spurious American fantasy of colorblindness, it is clear that as a young person he perceived racial differences, using all his senses to create a racial dividing line. How did Gates's contemporaries perceive the black community, and how central was the concept of race to their understanding of their social world? Wright's, Hurston's, and Gates's varied experiences make one wonder how central of a concern race was to most members of the privileged caste. If it was not always a consuming or determining factor for black southerners, like Gates and Hurston, how did white southerners, who were not members of an oppressed group, perceive and create Jim Crow reality? What impact did their racial identification have on their descriptions of life in the Jim Crow South? Were white perceptions of Jim Crow reality as divergent as African American descriptions of the era as represented by Wright, Hurston, and Gates? We will turn to the issue of white attempts to reconstruct the historical reality of Jim Crow in the next chapter.

CHAPTER FOUR

White Memoirists Remember Jim Crow

IN *North Toward Home* (1967), white Mississippian Willie Morris recounts having dinner with several civil rights activists in New York City in 1964. Morris, who had recently moved to New York to take a position at the prestigious *Harper's* magazine, had made a name for himself as a truly reconstructed southerner who was willing to acknowledge the brutality of the system of racial oppression in his native state. During the meal, one of his companions, a young African American woman from Mississippi, inexplicably started to sob and had to leave the table. Morris, who had overcome the racist indoctrination of his childhood to become a supporter of black civil rights, was shocked to learn that he was the source of her distress. Her friend explained, "You're the first Mississippi white person she was with socially. You made her nervous as hell."[1]

After that incident, Morris had a revelation. He realized that his Mississippi was quite simply a different Mississippi than the place the young woman knew. She had never experienced the tranquil Mississippi of his childhood, and he, despite his impeccable white liberal credentials, had never really visited her Mississippi, nor could he except through an act of empathetic imagination. Horrified, he finally understood: "The Mississippi these young people talked of was a different place from the one I had known, the things they said were not in context with mine; it was as if we were talking of another world—one that *looked* the same, that had the same place names, the same roads and rivers and landmarks, but beyond that the reality was awry, removed from my private reality of it" (380).

If the place-names and the landmarks that the civil rights worker discussed had not been so familiar, Morris, no doubt, would have denied that they were talking about the same geographical space. He could not transform his neighbors into the virulent defenders of white supremacy that his dinner companions both hated and feared. Now in his early thirties, Morris was more than a dozen years removed from a time when he actually resided in the state. He must have asked himself whether things had changed that much since his childhood. He must have wondered whether his Mississippi had devolved into such a loathsome place in the time that had elapsed since he left home. One can imagine the frenzied thoughts and explanations he must have considered as he tried to reconcile these competing Mississippis. How could he possibly reconcile the sentimental Mississippi of his childhood memories with this version of such an unremittingly hostile place?

Morris's epiphany has implications beyond his specific realization that his felt experience of life in Mississippi was much different from the felt experiences of the region's African Americans and of the civil rights workers. Every place, every time, every historical event is understood, interpreted, and experienced from any number of personal perspectives. We must remember that Morris's thoughts, perceptions, and feelings about Mississippi are as constitutive of the historical reality of Jim Crow as are the thoughts and feelings of the young black woman who had been so deeply traumatized by her Mississippi that she had unwittingly transformed Morris into a symbol of all that she hated and feared. Both versions of Mississippi are authentic ones, and if we are to endeavor to truly understand the time period, we must seek to understand both.

As we saw from an examination of Richard Wright's *Black Boy*, Zora Neale Hurston's *Dust Tracks on a Road*, and Henry Louis Gates Jr.'s *Colored People*, there is no definitive interpretation of the black Jim Crow experience. Wright's Mississippi bears a striking resemblance to the Mississippi described by the SNCC (Student Nonviolent Coordinating Committee) activists, but Hurston and Gates's South, while not as idyllic as Morris's, is hardly as bleak as Wright's. It should be no surprise, then, that white southerners, too, experienced, felt, and remembered Jim Crow in a wide variety of ways. Students of history must endeavor to understand, to rethink and refeel, these various Jim Crows if they are to come to a comprehensive understanding of the time period. Fortunately for the student of history, these complex and frequently contradictory Jim Crow worldviews are revealingly described in a number of literary memoirs that were written by autobiographers inhabiting varied subject positions.

This chapter examines Jim Crow as it was experienced and interpreted not only by Willie Morris but also by white southerners Lillian Smith and William Alexander Percy. Smith was an even more outspoken critic of the southern caste system than was Morris. Her memoir *Killers of the Dream* (1949) was written with the express purpose of critiquing racism, while *North Toward Home* was written for less polemical reasons. In the years since the publication of *Lanterns on the Levee* (1941), Percy has unwittingly been transformed into a representative example of a southern reactionary. However, this is not a label that his contemporaries would have applied to him. His very profound sense of noblesse oblige toward the black population made him suspect in the eyes of some of his white contemporaries. Nonetheless, he defended the southern caste system that Morris and Smith sought to dismantle.

All three memoirists root their Jim Crow memories within the larger context of southern history, demonstrating a desire to control not only the narrative voice of their own lives but also the way the history of their region is interpreted and remembered. Much like Wright, who strove to portray himself as a representative "black boy," Morris, Smith, and Percy all claim to be representative of a particular kind of southerner. All three endeavor to refute or complicate certain stereotypes about southern whiteness, and all three memoirists demonstrate a high degree of anxiety about what it meant to be a white southerner. In each text there are certain similarities, shared themes, and intersections of common thoughts about what it was like to be a white southerner in the segregated South. However, these memoirists differ in their political analyses of southern racism and in their degrees of willingness to share culpability for racial injustices.

Willie Morris, *North Toward Home*

Morris opens *North Toward Home* with a series of descriptions of his southern ancestors, proclaiming that his most revered ancestor was an uncle by marriage, Henry S. Foote, whom he considered a "true family hero" (10). Foote defeated Jefferson Davis in a gubernatorial election before the Civil War and steadfastly opposed secession. Morris proudly recalls that Foote's enemies "branded him a *pacifist*" (10). By invoking Foote's memory, Morris is claiming a legacy of southern moderation. He is writing himself into a vision of southern history that includes voices of restraint and tolerance. Morris does so in order to solve the dilemma he faces when he claims to love the Mississippi of his childhood while hating the firebrand Mississippians who had promoted and maintained racial inequality since the earliest days of white settlement in that geographical region.

Morris even makes light of certain conceptions of the venerated southern past. As a child, he enjoyed frightening his elderly aunts by reviving their Civil War memories. He would startle them, yelling, "*The Yankees are coming! . . .* Look at them horses! Look at them guns!" He never ceased to be amused at their alarm as they began scanning the road for signs of an occupying army. The Civil War was not the source of a painful memory to Morris as a child, and the myth of a glorious antebellum past did not guide his racial thinking when he was an adult. In neither case is he invested in a romantic vision of southern history. He is able to transform the tragic, Lost Cause version of the southern past into a laughing matter precisely because he was not dedicated to preserving white supremacy. Furthermore, Morris is able to find humor in the dark history of his region because he was not as negatively impacted by the past as were either the black victims of slavery and Jim Crow or the extreme white supremacists who were deeply invested in the system of racial oppression. When he was a child, the legacies of slavery, racism, and violence did not much trouble him because he was protected from them.

Like his ancestor Henry S. Foote, Morris chooses the only path left to him as he strives to place himself into the larger stream of southern history, the middle road. He is repulsed by moonlight-and-magnolias false memories of an idyllic South, but he cannot embrace a vision of southern history as completely pathological either. He cannot reconcile his childhood memories with such an unremittingly bleak vision of the southern past. After his conversation with the SNCC worker, he realizes that her Mississippi is actually a "different place." However, he cannot claim that version in its entirety, and thus he must create a narrative of the South that contains both discrimination and moderation, both happy childhood memories and racial atrocities.

Morris's memoir is historically revealing because he demonstrates how his perceptions and understanding of Jim Crow evolve throughout his life. He begins his account by describing his childhood acquiescence to the unreflective racism of his community and ends the book after having traveled many miles both geographically and ideologically from his roots. As we shall see, in contrast, Percy defends the southern way of life throughout his autobiography, and Smith recalls childhood events from the perspective of a mature narrator who does not approve of the way she was socialized into a racist society.

North Toward Home is divided into three sections, each taking a geographical name. As he moves geographically farther away from Mississippi, Morris's understanding of the region and of his own ethical and political sensibilities changes. The first section, "Mississippi," is an account of his childhood in a small town in the Yazoo Delta. The adult narrator lingers on the fringes of Morris's depiction of his childhood, ready to interject himself. On occasion the mature voice gingerly adds a bit of perspective to the experiences of his younger self. However, the older Morris is often deliberately mute. Unflinchingly, Morris describes his childhood as he experienced it, often resisting the temptation to apologize or to temper the racial insensitivity of his younger self. For example, when describing the euphoria of being "saved" at a religious revival meeting (a ritual that Morris participated in on more than one occasion), he remarks that afterwards "[he] would be tempted to embrace the first person [he] saw in the street, white or nigger" (39).

Morris's use of the racial epithet without ensconcing it in quotation marks or inserting a parenthetical disclaimer represents a deliberate choice, which was probably not an easy one to make for the sophisticated New York editor who wrote *North Toward Home*. At this moment in history in particular, one could gauge—to a relative degree of accuracy—the political sensibilities of white individuals according to the labels they used to describe the black population. Why did he consciously choose to use this despised and loaded term instead of his unfailingly polite (in the context of the time) usage of the word "Negro" (with a capital "N") in the rest of the text? By demonstrating how unfeelingly he dismissed and labeled the black inhabitants of his childhood world, Morris gives the reader an important insight into his felt reality. That is the word his younger self would have used. In deliberately employing it in his memoir, he is claiming this word and all that it evokes. He does this knowing that he is implicating his childhood self as a southern racist. Throughout the text, Morris takes his share of the culpability for Jim Crow racism straight up and is slow to make excuses for his behavior.

Later on, the mature Morris makes his attitude toward his black neighbors more explicit when he recalls his impervious childhood sense that "the

Negroes in the town were *there*: they were ours to do with what we wished" (78). Lillian Smith expresses a similar sentiment when she remarks that, although her childhood was permeated with religion and a constant fear of hell and sin, she soon learned that abusing African Americans was not sinful. She recalls, "You know you will not go to hell if you push little colored kids into sandspurs (or later out of jobs) though you may go there if you steal a nickel or do 'bad' things or even think of them."[2] As it turns out, Morris's childhood feelings about Jim Crow race rules and his perceptions of the black community were even more complicated than the intermingled contempt and dismissal implicit in his nonchalant use of the word "nigger."

During his Mississippi childhood, Morris found the black community mysterious and alluring, but the adults in his life stopped him from interacting with African Americans in any context that even approximated social equality. When he was a child, his mother forbade him to play with black children, and in his teenage years the local police consistently broke up the casual interracial football games that the local teenagers would organize (17–18, 82). However, these attempts to enforce social segregation only heightened the mystery and appeal that the black community held for Morris. Early in the text he refers to "that damp adventure and pulsing of blood of walking through niggertown alone" (7). Morris and his friends found the racial "other" so intriguing that around age thirteen he and his friends " 'went Negro' . . . trying to broaden [their] accents to sound like Negroes." He recalled, "We consciously walked like young Negroes, mocking their swinging gait" (81). The mature narrator does not interject himself to comment on the significance of his attempt to emulate what he saw as distinctly black behavior. From his brief description, it is impossible to know to what extent their actions stemmed from admiration and how much came from a cruel desire to mock people who were so little valued by the white community. However, it seems likely that both impulses were represented in their childish game of imitation.

Morris gives his readers a sense of his ambivalence about blackness when he describes watching baseball games with his father at the black high school. He recalls, "There was no condescension on our part, though the condescension might come later, if someone had asked where we had been. I would say, 'Oh, we been to see the nigger game' " (81). His internal impulse to watch the black team play baseball out of curiosity or even out of support for the athletes became transformed externally (once Morris was asked to account for it) into disdain. He demonstrates a willingness to let societal expectations shape or modify his inner thoughts as well as determine the value of his experiences.

Morris's feelings of interest in or respect for African Americans are fleeting. Unable to find a socially acceptable way to channel the natural feelings of camaraderie that sprang from living in such close proximity, he denies them. In one of the darkest passages in the text, he describes a capability toward violence that even his childhood self finds shameful:

> One summer morning when I was twelve, I sighted a little Negro boy walking with . . . his older sister. . . . The little boy could not have been more than about three. . . .
>
> Just as he got in front of me, lurking . . . in the bushes, I jumped out and pounced upon him. I slapped him across the face, kicked him with my knee, and with a shove sent him sprawling on the concrete. (77)

When presenting this incident of childhood cruelty, Morris again resists the temptation to interpret his actions, to provide broad sociological explanations for why he unfeelingly harmed that African American toddler. In presenting the incident this way, he captures the felt experience of his Mississippi childhood. As a boy he acted on impulses he did not understand. After this incident he was left with intermingled feelings of exhilaration and shame, which were inexplicable to his childhood self.

The voice of the mature narrator does interject itself to comment that his "conduct with Negroes . . . was a relationship of contrasts" (a statement made obvious by his evidence in the text). However, he does not try to explain the root of his profound ambivalence (78). By presenting but not explaining his behavior, Morris captures how his childhood self felt. He experienced great swings of emotion about the southern racial system, to which his erratic behavior was a response. Clearly, as a child he was not self-aware enough to probe the causes for his actions or to reflect deeply on southern race relations. Rather, he responded to the world as he found it. He had inherited a sense of racial privilege and entitlement, which seemingly justified all his behavior. He did not pursue the matter any further until he achieved geographical distance from his home and the emotional maturity to understand it.

Although the issue of race relations (and Morris's accompanying implicit confessions of racism) is an important theme in the book, the memoir is not about race relations, strictly speaking. Morris writes about his family, his love of baseball, his dating experiences, and his beloved dog, among other things. The issue of race surfaces frequently because, after all, state-sanctioned racism is the defining characteristic of the segregated Deep South. A sensitive memoirist trying to capture the spirit of his or her time could simply not avoid the subject. However, it comes into focus fleetingly and is lost again among fond recollections of Morris's grandfather or of his love of the Mississippi landscape. In his childhood memories, all these impressions are intermingled. While animosity toward whites is the central focus of *Black Boy*, race relations are not always central in *North Toward Home*. Morris bravely acknowledges that he, too, can be implicated for southern racism, but he does not pretend that this awareness haunted him as a child. Nor does his future enlightenment about racial issues dampen his other childhood memories or the love he feels for the state of Mississippi.

While Smith, as we shall see, endeavors to analyze the roots of southern racism, Morris first accepts Jim Crow values and later rejects them without an explicit critique. If *North Toward Home* were a work of fiction, it would likely include foreshadowing of Morris's racial conversion. Perhaps a dramatic sequence of actions would result in an epiphany for the protagonist accompanied by lyrical passages about the brotherhood of all humankind. Maybe a dream sequence would reveal that the narrator was subconsciously tortured by his southern racism and all that it entailed. There are any number of ways that an author of fiction could reveal the intellectual shift that took place in the Morris character.

However, because this is a memoir, because Morris is using literary art to capture his felt experience, he does not resort to such blatant fictional techniques—however satisfying they might be to a reader in search of dramatic structure and a plausible explanation for Jim Crow cruelties. A reader of his memoir in search of foreshadowing might note that as a child Morris had ambivalent feelings about African Americans. However, his pronounced tendency was to view the region's black inhabitants with amusement or scorn. His childish attitudes do not portend a racial awakening in the future.

Morris unflinchingly acknowledges that at the age of seventeen he wanted to be a Mississippi planter, a fantasy made more concrete because his girlfriend—a blond majorette from his high school—was the daughter of a prominent local planter. Again, we hear the voice of the mature narrator as Morris scornfully recalls: "I had my heart set . . . on entering

Mississippi's educated landed gentry—by taking a degree at Ole Miss, as all my friends planned to do, and by returning to that plantation with my majorette, to preside there on the banks of the Yazoo over boll weevils big enough to wear dog tags [and] pre–Earl Warren darkies. . . . I knew Mississippi and I loved what I saw" (140–41).

Morris ultimately abandons this loaded daydream, instead leaving his native state to enroll at the University of Texas. In abandoning his earlier vision of himself he does not recall being propelled by intellectual curiosity or a desire to see a broader world. His father advised him to leave Mississippi in search of greater opportunity. However, it is unclear whether his father's advice alone was sufficient to transform his fantasy of his future life. Even in retrospect Morris is not sure what made him leave Mississippi. He muses, "In trying to recapture a turning point in one's life at such an age, it is almost impossible to ascribe tangible motives to some great change in one's direction, to isolate a thought, or a decision" (143). Whatever his motivations, his decision to enroll in the University of Texas was a fateful one.

The second section of *North Toward Home* is "Texas." Morris describes his college days, which were characterized by his growing "acceptance of ideas themselves as something worth living by" (150). Morris's intellectual awakening is swift, and the change he goes through is irrevocable. As editor of the university's student newspaper, Morris gained a reputation as something of a social progressive for his willingness to challenge the administration and the social conservatism of the 1950s. Shortly after the *Brown v. Board of Education* decision, he daringly proclaimed that the University of Texas was ready for integration (177).

After graduation, he studied at Oxford on a Rhodes fellowship. Afterward, he returned to Texas to write for and later edit the *Texas Observer*, a newspaper that had been founded in 1954 as an alternative to the mainstream press in Texas. While Morris was with the newspaper, his editorials championed the cause of the poor and racial and ethnic minorities. He also published an exposé about the John Birch Society and provided relentless critiques of Texas politicians. This second section of *North Toward Home* demonstrates that Morris had indeed become (to use his language) a "converted southern boy" (378). In defiance of reader expectations, Morris is not explicit about the moment of his conversion. Fred Hobson observes that Morris never delivers "one great moment of awakening, a time when the magnitude of all those sins became clear."[3] He does not offer the reader an altar call scene like the one he describes as a child when he went to the front of the church to repent of his sins and be saved.

During the summer of 1955, right before the start of his senior year at the University of Texas, Morris returned briefly to Mississippi. He describes an event during that trip to demonstrate how his old childhood sensibilities collided with the new political and ethical beliefs he had adopted since leaving home. Morris arrived home to Yazoo City to find his neighbors embroiled in the fallout from the 1954 Supreme Court decision that had declared segregated schools unconstitutional. Backed by the National Association for the Advancement of Colored People, more than fifty of the town's black residents had signed a petition calling for the integration of the local schools. Infuriated, the white community began to organize in opposition.

One night Morris attended a meeting, which had been called to discuss strategies for preventing the integration of the local schools. So many of the town's residents turned out for the inaugural meeting of the White Citizens Council that Morris was forced to park several blocks away. When he arrived at the meeting, tensions were high. The "pent-up hysteria" in the room made Morris uneasy (178). As the meeting progressed, Morris's former neighbors made the decision to retaliate against the African Americans who had signed the petition by firing them from their jobs, refusing to sell them groceries, and evicting them from rental property. Some of those assembled preferred to resort to violence, and Morris heard the sounds of racial epithets and rebel yells. However, the majority of the crowd, the "respectable" members of society, overruled overt violence, preferring other forms of coercion instead. At one point in the proceedings, a man who owned a house across the street from the Morris home stood up and spoke. He expressed his approval for the spirit of the plans formulated that evening but expressed doubts about the constitutionality of those measures. However, the crowd was not in the mood for a lesson about the U.S. Constitution that night, and Morris's neighbor was silenced. As Fred Hobson observes, if Morris had a single racial epiphany at all, he had it at that moment:

> I sat there, quiet as could be. For a brief moment I was tempted to stand up and support my neighbor, but I lacked the elemental courage to go against that mob. For it *was* a mob, and I was not the same person I had

been three years before. In the pit of my stomach, I felt a strange and terrible disgust. I looked back and saw my father, sitting still and gazing straight ahead; on the stage my friends' fathers nodded their heads and talked among themselves. I felt an urge to get out of there. *Who were these people?* I asked myself. What was I doing there? Was this the place I had grown up in and never wanted to leave? I knew in that instant, in the middle of a mob in our school auditorium, that a mere three years in Texas had taken me irrevocably, even without my recognizing it, from home. (179–80)

In that moment Morris faces the fact that he has changed. However, what brought about that change seems to be as unclear to him as it is to the reader. This was the nature of Morris's racial awakening as he experienced it. He didn't have a single moment of revelation. Instead he had slowly, imperceptibly come to a new understanding of the world around him. To refeel Morris's Jim Crow experience is to accompany him in the transformation from a child oblivious to racial injustices to a young man newly sensitized but unable as yet to speak his newfound beliefs in the setting of his childhood world.

Although Morris's time in Texas had been fruitful professionally as well as intellectually, he never became as emotionally attached to the state as he had been to Mississippi. However, he found that he was literally and figuratively unable to return home. In 1963, his burgeoning career as a talented young editor brought him to New York City. "New York," the last section of *North Toward Home*, recalls his experiences in the big city. The move had a tremendous impact on his career. He landed a coveted job at *Harper's*, becoming the youngest-ever editor in chief of the magazine in 1967, the same year his memoir appeared. Morris discovered that his socialization into the ways of Jim Crow experiences had marked him, and he filtered all subsequent experiences through his conception of himself as a "converted southern boy."

He found it difficult to conceive of himself both as a southerner and as a liberal on racial issues. In the world he had come from these two qualities seldom existed side by side and seemed in opposition. His decision to move to New York was one effort to respond to this tension. He attempted to escape from these contradictions but found he could not. Morris figured himself as an exile, forever haunted by his past: "Mississippi may have been the only state in the Union (or certainly one of a half dozen in the South) which had produced a genuine set of exiles . . . alienated from home but forever drawn back to it, seeking some form of personal liberty elsewhere yet obsessed with the texture and complexity of the place from which they had departed" (320).

However, geographical distance from the South did not free Morris from the complicated feelings he had about the region. His choice of the title *North Toward Home* is far too optimistic. It is clear, even as he is writing his memoir, that Morris hasn't managed to convince himself that he has found a new home. Biographical information about him reveals that Morris eventually made his peace with Mississippi after the civil rights movement ended. In 1980 he returned to that state as writer-in-residence at the University of Mississippi and lived in Mississippi for the rest of his life. The last chapter of the second volume of his autobiography, *New York Days* (1993), is aptly titled "South toward Home."

Morris captures the felt experience of a southern liberal who cannot reject his fond childhood memories of Mississippi, his love for his family, and his sentimental attachment to his hometown. However, these memories are tainted by his awareness of the racial injustices of the region. For Morris these complex emotions about Mississippi are intermingled. To refeel Morris's Jim Crow experience is to feel his ambivalence and his anxiety about his identity as a white southerner. At one point, he goes so far as to deny his southern roots in an attempt to escape his internal dilemma. One day when a New York editor asked him where he was from, he shocked himself by answering, "Northern California" (363).

The virulence of northern racism does not escape Morris. However, as a southerner he feels a particular duty to speak out against racism. Again and again the issue resurfaces long after he has left the South. One day while riding the subway, Morris accidentally bumped into a black man. Their exchange was colored by their initial perceptions of each other, which were the outgrowth of their respective Jim Crow experiences:

> "I'm sorry," I said. "I didn't have anything to hold on to. This is a hell of a way to live."
>
> "It beats them hills, don't it?" the man said, in a strong Negro Southern accent.

"What hills?" I asked.

"Them hills you come from with that cracker accent."

"If I wasn't a liberal I'd hit you for that," I said. . . .

"Hell, ain't *nobody* liberal," the man said. "Who's liberal?"

"Well, I'm not from the hills, I'm from Mississippi."

"The *mud* then. Don't this beat the mud?"

"The mud's dried."

"Wait till spring," he said. "Then it'll be mud again."

We stared wordlessly at each other, two sons of the South. . . . Finally, at the next stop, ashamed and a little guilty, I clawed my way out. (348)

In this impasse on the subway, Morris succinctly reveals the extent to which his Jim Crow reality had differed from that of the black man he encountered. Although they were both "sons of the South," as Morris observed, their inside perceptions of the Jim Crow South and thus of each other as southerners differed drastically. The black man on the subway was likely accustomed to being mistreated by southern white men, while Morris grew up expecting "that Negro adults, even Negro adults I encountered alone and had never seen before, would treat me with generosity and affection" (78). The Jim Crow experiences of one man primed him to expect hostility, while the other man's experiences led him to expect deference. In both cases, their expectations were somewhat disappointed, highlighting the complexity of actual experience in contrast to attempts to impose a narrative full of stock characters and formulaic narratives onto nuanced, contradictory historical realities.

When the African American man heard Morris's southern accent, his reflexive response was one of hostility. He called Morris a "cracker" because his accent probably brought back memories of countless unpleasant encounters with other white southerners. He viewed Morris with suspicion and as guilty by association from the first syllable of the conversation. Morris, however, instead of playing the part of the sensitive white liberal he fancied himself, returned the man's hostility in kind. In the heat of the moment he seemed to forget that the man he was speaking with had likely suffered from Jim Crow injustices of the kind that Morris himself had meted out. Morris may temporarily have forgotten that the man's hostility and suspicion were historically justified. Instead of empathizing with the man and feeling the weight of their collective history, Morris actually used his "liberalism" as a weapon. He was using his politics as an excuse for not striking the man and at the same time letting him know that Morris believed he deserved to be struck. There is also an undertone of pride in Morris's announcement that he is a "liberal"; it is as if he hopes to shame the black man for not immediately recognizing Morris as a man of enlightened sensibilities. Morris's instinctively defensive and hostile reaction in this encounter seems to validate the black man's suspicion that there is no such thing as a "liberal." It is no wonder, then, that Morris walks away from the encounter feeling "ashamed and a little guilty."

Just as Morris could not traverse the distance between himself and the man on the subway, he also found himself reluctant to correspond with his fellow Mississippian Richard Wright. Morris met Wright in Paris in 1957, but when Wright expressed interest in corresponding, Morris could not bring himself to write. Analyzing his hesitation, he claims, "Partly my reluctance had been due to a lack of self-confidence, that a 'liberated' small-town Mississippi boy has anything unusual to offer this 'liberated' Southern Negro writer of an older generation. But also I think it was due to my feeling that Wright, in many ways so admirable a man, was so different from me in temperament and loyalty and experience that we had almost nothing in common" (383–84). As peculiar as his explanation sounds for the fact that (at the beginning of his career) he refused to correspond with an internationally famous writer, it may be an accurate one. Morris sensed that the gulf between himself and Wright, specifically their different historical understandings of Jim Crow, could not be traversed. To try to bridge the gap would have been too painful for Morris.

Morris could never succeed in reconciling his Mississippi with that of the SNCC workers, his Mississippi with Wright's Mississippi. What he sentimentally felt and what he intellectually knew continued to coexist uneasily. Forgetting himself when he met a SNCC worker from Texas one day, his parting words were, "Think of me next time you're in Yazoo." Unflinchingly she replied, "Think of it yourself, you son-of-a-bitch. . . . It's your hometown not mine" (381). Morris was certainly not the only white southerner who felt conflicted about violating the region's racial mores. The stakes for speaking out were high. Lillian Smith, one of the most outspoken critics of southern racism, also felt the tension between what her conscience dictated and what the southern social order demanded.

Lillian Smith, *Killers of the Dream*

When reading *North Toward Home*, the reader has the impression that the issue of race keeps rearing itself almost against the author's will. When reflecting on his past while living in New York, Morris somewhat plaintively observes, "And always there were the Negroes, the white Southerner's awareness of them. . . . *Always the Negroes*" (376–77). The burden of guilt and responsibility that Morris feels is sometimes too much for him. In contrast, in Lillian Smith's *Killers of the Dream*, racism is not just one theme that runs through her memoir. It is *the* theme. While the issue of race creeps into Morris's recollections almost in spite of himself, the opposite is true in Smith's case. She set out to write a book about race, and some autobiographical material crept in. The end result is a unique kind of life writing. Smith does not adhere to a strict chronology. She doesn't cover the typical autobiographical bases. The reader is not presented with anecdotes about high school and college or stories about ambitions realized or thwarted. Smith reveals only autobiographical information concerning the way that she (and by extension other southerners) was socialized into a society that she believes is dysfunctional. Unlike Morris, Smith does not try to capture the sensibility of her childhood self. The voice of the mature narrator is the dominant one, and she filters her childhood experiences through an adult perspective.

Like Morris, Smith also endeavors to tell the biography of her region. She embeds her own life story within southern history, which she tells in bits and pieces in several chapters. She utilizes both sweeping narratives and parables to describe the southern past. Smith saw her rendering of southern history as an alternative to the nostalgic version of the southern past presented by her contemporaries, the Agrarians and the Fugitive poets. Smith also analyzes the toll that racism had taken on many of the region's inhabitants, particularly on white women. According to Will Brantley, "Smith assumes Freud's role as psychoanalyst, as therapist, she isolates the sources of the South's psychosis in order to offer, if at times obliquely, a way of healing."[4] Smith interjects her own life story only by way of example, as a case study of the impact that Jim Crow mores had on all the region's white inhabitants.

Lillian Smith was born in 1897 into a prosperous family living in a small Florida town. In 1915, after the family business failed, the family moved into its summer cottage on Old Screamer Mountain in Clayton, Georgia. The Smiths made their living first by running an inn and later a girls' summer camp on the mountainside property. As a young woman, Lillian briefly studied both at Piedmont College and at the Peabody Conservatory of Music in Baltimore, Maryland. However, the most transformational moment of her life came in 1922 when she accepted a position teaching music at the Virginia School in Huchow, China. Her time in China proved to be intellectually stimulating as she began to read Eastern philosophy. Even more important, she became more politically and socially engaged as a result of her time spent overseas. She was appalled by the poverty she saw in China and became increasingly interested in global affairs, seeing parallels between the havoc wrought by European colonialism abroad and southern racism back at home in Georgia.[5]

Upon returning home, Smith helped her parents run the Laurel Falls Camp, putting more and more of her imprint on the programming and eventually taking over altogether. While working at the camp, Smith met Paula Snelling, who was to become her lifelong companion, collaborator, and lover.[6] The fact of Smith's carefully closeted sexual identity has led many to speculate that her own feelings of marginalization might have led her empathize so strongly with the plight of the disinherited in the South.

Whether or not this is the case, her relationship with Snelling proved to be personally satisfying and professionally productive. From 1936 to 1945, the two founded and ran a small magazine known first as *Pseudopodia* and later as *South Today*, hoping to give voice to talented and progressive southerners, including blacks. In 1944, her novel *Strange Fruit*, which chronicled an interracial relationship, appeared to much controversy, making Smith famous as a champion for the cause of racial tolerance and integration. Her autobiography was an attempt to continue this work.

Smith is not coy about her motives in writing *Killers of the Dream*. She wants to indict southern pathology and to convince the region's inhabitants to mend their ways. Because of her highly politicized agenda, some readers of *Killers of the Dream* might view Smith's observations with suspicion. Even to a greater extent than Wright, Smith makes it clear that she is writing a polemic. However, we must keep in mind that all memoirists are waging a war for the historical memory of their readers—whether or not they are consciously aware of doing so. In a certain sense, Smith does her readers a favor by explicitly stating her motivations. Her interpretations of her culture and of her childhood are indelibly imprinted with her political position, and she is self-aware enough to acknowledge this influence.

Interestingly, Smith does not appeal to white southerners, asking them to reform on purely altruistic grounds. She urges them to abandon the Jim Crow system because of the damage it does to the white as well as the black community. Fred Hobson has observed that "to a black reader of *Killers of the Dream*—as, indeed, with most white conversion narratives— the author's thinking might have seemed somewhat self indulgent. That is, attaining psychic wholeness for whites sometimes seemed for Smith to be at least as important as attaining equal rights for blacks."[7] At one point Smith stunningly declares that southern women "dimly realized" that the southern way of life "had injured themselves and their children as much as it had injured the Negro" (146–47).

Like Wright, Smith puts her own personal experiences at the center of her understanding of Jim Crow, extrapolating from her own life story that southern racism had psychologically injured the white community. Smith had been wounded both by being raised as a racist and as a result of her attempts to speak out against racism. Not only did many southerners revile her for daring, in *Strange Fruit*, to fictionally depict interracial love, but the book also holds the dubious distinction of having been banned in Boston because of complaints about obscenity.[8] Smith's notoriety was a mixed blessing because she certainly became famous as a result of the bad press and enjoyed some aspects of her newfound fame. However, at times she could not help but feel singed by the negative publicity. She became convinced that the literary establishment was punishing her for her immoderate views—both by closing off avenues for publication and by failing to take her seriously as an artist. She claimed that the failure of the intelligentsia to treat her like a "good and serious writer" was the "hurt of [her] life."[9]

Smith also remained fearful of reprisals other than ostracism. When fire destroyed her bedroom and study at Old Screamer, two white juvenile delinquents were accused of the crime but left the state and did not face trial. Smith understandably felt that the crime may have been "mixed . . . with feelings about [her] and [her] work."[10] Thus, it is no surprise that Smith felt that she, too, had suffered as a result of Jim Crow.

Like Smith, Wright also believed that both whites and blacks were damaged by the institutionalization of southern racism, but his sympathy is clearly with the victims of white oppression. Smith's perspective is unusual because of her surprising assertion that whites and blacks had been equally victimized, and her Jim Crow memories must be understood accordingly. According to Smith, "what cruelly shapes and cripples the personality of one is as cruelly shaping and crippling the personality of the other" (39).

Smith's strong statements equating white and black suffering may, in part, represent a rhetorical strategy, a compelling argument to convince her white readers to mend their ways for their own good. However, this position also stems from Smith's own Jim Crow experiences, the inside of her historical moment. Although she tries to imagine what impact Jim Crow must have had on African Americans, she cannot concretely comprehend the social reality of Jim Crow from black perspectives. She can, however, understand the toll Jim Crow took on her own development. She also knows—though less concretely—the strain that living under and maintaining the Jim Crow social order has had on her friends and family in the white community. In Smith's opinion, the impact has been devastating.

Although most of Smith's moral outrage is directed at state-sanctioned southern racism, she is also critical of fundamentalist Christianity. The brand of religion that she was taught as a child placed an enormous emphasis on sin, particularly sexual sins. Thus Smith and other children from her community learned that masturbation was a vile, if not unpardonable, sin. However, mistreating African Americans, if at all sinful, was not a very serious infraction. According to Smith, this skewed version of Christianity, which taught but did not practice the doctrine of loving one's neighbor, produced a generation of southern hypocrites. In her estimation, the separation of doctrine from practice caused the southern mind to "split." In her analysis the gash was "hardly more than a crack at first, but we began in those early years a two-leveled existence which we have since managed quite smoothly" (84). Thus, Smith uses autobiographical material to document the toll Jim Crow took on her ability to think freely and her instinct to embrace her fellow humans. She then goes on to speculate about how those in the South might go about repairing these cracks in their white, southern psyche.

Smith singles out white women as among Jim Crow's most put upon victims. According to Smith, the relationships between white men and black women and white children and black mammy figures devalued white women, leaving them powerless and isolated. She extends sympathy to white women who, in her analysis, were figuratively put on pedestals but stripped of actual power. She claims, "All a women can expect from lingering on exalted heights is a hard chill afterwards" (143). A number of questions, if not outright objections, can be raised regarding Smith's depiction of white women as victims. Although there is almost certainly more than a kernel of truth in her observations, her overwhelming sympathy for the white woman also strips them of some of the culpability for creating and maintaining the Jim Crow system.

Smith's analysis also seems directed primarily at middle- or upper-class women with enough resources to pay a black woman to care for their children. Smith believed, "Of all the humiliating experiences which southern white women have endured, the least easy to accept, I think, was that of a mother who had no choice but to take the husk of a love which her son in his earliest years had given to another woman" (138). This scenario was clearly not applicable to white women who worked, for example, in textile mills or as tenant farmers. Many of these women lacked the resources to provide many basic necessities for their children and certainly were not in the economic position to hire nurses to care for them. Smith's expression of sympathy for middle-class women may suggest that she was more adept at transcending the political implications of racial identification than she was at critiquing class issues.

Regardless of the potential objections that can be raised to her analyses, Smith's discussion of white victimization under Jim Crow is very revealing. When reading a memoir as a historical resource, we are generally not looking for a historical or sociological overview of a historical moment. Smith provides these things—albeit in a personal rather than a scholarly fashion. One could certainly read *Killers of the Dream* for the express purpose of evaluating her arguments on their merits. However, in general, the historical study of memoirs reveals how an author experienced, perceived, and remembered her or his historical moment. With this in mind, our primary question is not whether we agree with Smith. Rather, we are interested in how she felt and what that tells us about Jim Crow reality from her perspective.

Lillian Smith was such an outspoken critic of southern segregation and racism that she was viewed with suspicion by many of the other so-called liberals of her day. When she began speaking out on issues of race in the 1930s, southern "liberalism" was frequently defined merely as speaking out against racial violence or demanding that separate accommodations actually be brought up to the equality dictated by the "separate but equal" formula of the era. In contrast, Smith called for an immediate end to southern segregation. As a result of her uncompromising principles, she was ostracized by many members of the white community as well as by the literary establishment. Throughout her life, she complained that, despite having written the best-selling novel *Strange Fruit*, she had garnered little interest or respect for her subsequent efforts.

When reading *Killers of the Dream* for historical insights and attempting to refeel the past moment from Smith's perspective, one should keep in mind that she represents a political extreme for her day. That being said, her emphasis on the impact of Jim Crow on whites might seem surprising to contemporary readers of the text who, rightfully, place the victimization of black southerners at the center of their understanding of the time period in question. It is important to remember that in her case Jim Crow racism and her decision to speak out against it did take an enormous toll on her. Perhaps the extent of her own personal suffering explains her position that whites and blacks suffered equally under southern segregation.

It is also significant that her unconventional decision to speak out against racism did not free her from maintaining many beliefs that indicate an unconscious racism on her part. *Killers of the Dream* is rife with stereotypical images of blackness. Her complex and sometimes contradictory viewpoints are an outgrowth of her peculiar environment and represent one potential way that white southerners could have responded to Jim Crow. In our attempts to understand the era of segregation, it is too simplistic to label some southerners, like Smith, as racial "liberals" and others, like Percy, as "conservatives." To accurately refeel this past moment from these various perspectives, we must delve deeper and develop an understanding that embraces the true complexity of these individual points of view.

Although the primary goal of *Killers of the Dream* is to champion the cause of equality of African Americans, Smith's descriptions of black people are frequently one-dimensional and stereotypical. Unwittingly Smith makes a case for racial difference not completely unlike that advanced by proponents of the southern caste system. Thus at times Smith appears caught between what her conscience dictates and what her culture has taught her to believe. When describing the enslaved population she declares: "From all that we know of them they seem to have had, even as some do now, a marvelous love of life and play, a physical grace and rhythm and a psychosexual vigor that must have made the white race by contrast seem washed-out and drained of much that is good and life-giving" (117). Her sweeping generalizations about blacks in the plantation setting as well as during the Jim Crow era do not end there. She claims that black children had "an exuberance, and a lack of sadism and guilt that no Anglo-Saxon group, to my knowledge, has ever shown." She repeatedly embraces essentialist ideas about blackness, furthermore arguing, "Throughout the ordeal of slavery they remained people of easy dignity, kindly, humorous. . . . They developed severe faults, of course, during those centuries. Easy lying, deceit, flattery" (118). Smith tells us that after emancipation the mammy figure maintained a "biologically rooted humor" (129). As we shall see, Smith's depiction of black southerners is quite similar to that of William Alexander Percy, an avowed southern conservative.

No doubt Smith intended her descriptions of African Americans to be positive and to elicit white sympathy for what she describes as a cheerful and long-suffering group of people. She also, if inadvertently, describes African Americans as somewhat simpleminded. Smith recalls knowing many "strong old women—the children of slaves," whom she claims to have known intimately enough to be able to declare that they did not suffer "from that sickness of the soul we call ambivalence" (119). It seems that Smith could not believe that these elderly figures she remembered from her childhood could have the some kind of complicated and sometimes contradictory thoughts and emotions that she had. If she could feel conflicted between love of her region and her criticisms of it, could not these black women have felt similarly torn?

When wondering about how blacks might have dealt with Jim Crow cruelty, again we get insight into Smith's perceptions of the world of Jim Crow and its inhabitants. She speculates, "I think maybe they drew a little circle around their small personal lives and tried not to look beyond. . . . They lived in these small lives with work and raising their families and their hope of heaven and a struggle for education, and dancing and razor fights and dreams and laughter" (69). In retrospect, and in light of Wright's and Hurston's memoirs, it seems that Smith suffered from a lack of empathetic imagination about felt experience from African American perspectives. By developing an understanding of the way Smith misperceived her social reality, we can come to a deeper understanding of the behavior of other southern whites who held similar misperceptions.

From Smith's perspective, segregation, black disenfranchisement, and racial violence were wrong. However, she implicitly makes clear that she also believes there are inherent racial differences between whites and blacks. In her estimation many of these differences, such as mammy's "biologically rooted humor," are admirable, but there are differences nonetheless. To refeel the inside of her historical moment and to view the social reality of Jim Crow from her perspective is to feel intermingled pity and condescension for the black population. Given that perspective, is it any wonder that Smith reserves much of her sympathy for the white population? In her estimation the white population is, after all, haunted by "ambivalence." This being the case, she might surmise that whites might actually suffer more than the somewhat simpleminded blacks at whom racial violence and segregation were actually directed.

Like Morris, Smith views Jim Crow through a complicated set of contradictory thoughts, feelings, and loyalties. She loves her family and her community, and she hates racism. However, her family and her community are part of the racist social order that she despises. Can she find a way to hate racism but not her family and her community? This dilemma might explain why Smith makes the unsubstantiated and rather bizarre claim that "there are only two or three million of these racists—the other segregationists are simply conformists" (18). This is a distinction that Wright may not have been able to appreciate, but for Smith it is crucial. She is scornful of southern conformists but spares this group from the wrath she reserves for the actual racists. She chooses to believe, "Our mothers and fathers would have weakened, I think, had not religion and southern tradition kept them hard at the teaching" (93). Ultimately she puts the blame for the entire social order at the doorstep of a minority of the population, letting the majority of white southerners, who by both their actions and their inaction supported and perpetuated institutionalized discrimination, off the hook.

Smith uses her skills as a creative writer to distill the essence of her childhood experiences into a few revealing episodes, arguing that these and other memories are "never quite facts but sometimes closer to the 'truth' than any fact" (13). The episodes she recalls from her childhood are full of contradictory and confusing messages, which even as an adult she seems incapable of completely untangling. She remains perpetually mystified that "the mother who taught me what I know of tenderness and love and compassion taught me also the bleak rituals of keeping Negroes in their 'place.' The father who rebuked me for an air of superiority toward schoolmates from the mill and rounded out his rebuke by gravely reminding me that 'all men are brothers,' trained me in the steel-rigid decorums that I must demand of every colored male" (27). She expresses this same sort of puzzlement over the contradictory lessons that she learned as a child while interacting with other adults: "You knew your father's friends did use the sweat box or stocks or whipping as punishment for the convicts leased out to them and these same friends gave you and your little sister candy and dimes" (71). Like Morris, Smith has so much difficulty reconciling these southern contradictions that at times she would prefer not even to try. She mourns, "There is too much that made me love the place where I was born, that makes me even now want to remember only the good things" (71).

As a child, Smith seemed to vacillate between guilt and an unthinking acquiescence to the dictates of the southern social order. Like Morris, Smith was profoundly affected by evangelical Christianity as a child. Her religious training seems to have both heightened and confused her childhood feelings of guilt, which stemmed not only from questions about Jim Crow racism but also from anxiety about sexual behavior. Smith remembers attending revival meetings in which a traveling preacher would prey on the emotions of the people in the audience, warning them about hell and damnation while luring them to the altar with carefully selected hymns. Like Morris, Smith found the altar call irresistible: "I went up to the altar and stayed until the revivalist pried me off my knees, I was never convinced that my kneeling had effected a change in either my present or my future life. But sometimes, wanting it so badly, I lied and stood up with the rest when the evangelist asked all who were sure they would go to heaven to arise and be counted. My younger sister, more certain of her place in the family, was naturally more certain of her place in heaven, and rarely went to the altar. I remember how I admired her restraint" (110). In this passage, Smith capitalizes on the connections she has previously made between religion and racism. She is aware that, although she is particularly haunted by the complexity and contradictions surrounding these issues, not all southerners share her pain and confusion equally. She is tormented by the haunting fear that she has not been saved and may indeed not be redeemable. Her sister, however, is not plagued by these fears and is able to resist the emotive release of the altar call. Smith knows that her perceptions of Jim Crow, the inside of her historical moment, are different even from those of her sister, with whom she shared so much.

The mature narrator does not claim that she was riddled with guilt every moment of her childhood. She describes her Jim Crow experiences as occurring on two levels. Some moments she was riddled with anxiety and shame, and at other times she navigated her cultural terrain without thinking, as if she were on autopilot. Much of the time she uncritically bowed to Jim Crow custom. She recalls, "I don't think we noticed the signs. Somehow we seemed always to walk through the right door. People find it hard to question something that has been here since they were born" (57). Jay Watson claims that Smith effectively demonstrates that southern "rituals become progressively internalized, white Southerners can practice segregation without the need for any legitimating ideas at all. They simply live their ideology, to their benefit and detriment at once, without thinking about it at all."[11] Smith is able to capture compellingly a fractured southern experience. Sometimes she questioned the southern racial system and was conscious of being complicit in an enormous wrong being perpetrated on a societal level. Other times, even most of the time, she unconsciously behaved the way her society demanded. Both the painful pangs of conscience and the unthinking adherence to Jim Crow dictates were part of her experience.

The system of segregation left such a deep imprint on Smith that it served as a powerful metaphor in various aspects of her life. The metaphor of segregation was used to characterize the powerful societal taboo against sexual experimentation outside the institution of marriage. Smith recalls learning, "Now, parts of your body are segregated areas which you must stay away from and keep others away from. These areas you touch only when necessary. In other words, you cannot associate freely with them any more than you can associate freely with colored children" (87). Smith's childhood was governed by the metaphor of segregation, and she spent her young life consciously and otherwise seeking socially sanctioned spaces to occupy. Using her skill as a writer, she demonstrated what a powerful controlling idea segregation was. The terror of violating the strictures of segregation was an overwhelming one, and as a result, anxiety about segregation spilled out beyond the southern racial situation.

If segregation proved to be such a powerful conceptual framework that Smith practiced it without thinking, even going so far as to apply the metaphor of segregation to matters that were not race-related, how was she able to think her way outside it? Morris, as we saw, was not able to pinpoint a single moment of revelation in his growing criticism of Jim Crow. Watson argues that "in [Smith's] world doors occasionally open. There are things people can do" to escape the ideology of their culture.[12] Smith identifies a number of events in her childhood that caused her temporarily to question the ethics of Jim Crow. The most powerful incident involved a young girl whom Smith's parents briefly considered adopting.

One day Smith's mother received word from some concerned towns-women that a white child had been found living with a black family. Against this family's wishes, young "Janie" was taken from their custody and brought to live with the Smith family. She remained there for three weeks, sleeping in young Lillian's bed, wearing her clothes, and sitting be-side her at meals. Their developing friendship was interrupted when word came from an orphanage that, despite Janie's light complexion, she had an African American parent. Immediately, Smith's mother decided that Janie must leave the home.

Lillian was upset and confused at her mother's explanation that Janie had to leave because she was "a little colored girl." Young Lillian felt guilt both because she knew that Janie was being mistreated and because in living alongside a black child she had violated a strict social taboo. At the time, Smith felt compelled to believe that her parents were right, remembering, "It was the only way my world could be held together" (37–38). Nonetheless, doubts lingered and multiplied, and Smith gradually began to reject Jim Crow and try to change the way her social reality was constituted.

As with Smith and Morris, Jim Crow race relations were a source of tremendous anxiety for William Alexander Percy. However, while both Smith and Morris interpreted their anxiety and ambivalence as a sign that something was wrong with the social order, Percy took the opposite ap-proach. He believed that institutionalized white supremacy was the only effective way the South could be governed. He attributed his unease to the fact that times were changing, believing that in many respects southern society had been steadily deteriorating since the end of slavery.

William Alexander Percy, *Lanterns on the Levee*

William Alexander Percy was born in 1885 into a prominent Mississippi family of plantation owners. His charismatic and well-connected father,

LeRoy Percy, had served as U.S. senator. Like Morris and Smith, Percy embeds his own life story in the larger story of southern history. His version of the southern past is reminiscent of the plantation school of thought. His ancestors were unfailingly brave and noble. In his imagination, the antebellum past represented a better era, and things had been deteriorating ever since. He sadly observes, "Our Delta Culture stemmed from an older one and returned to it for sustenance and renewal, but it lacked much that made the older culture charming and stable."[13] Although Percy owned a plantation at the time he wrote his autobiography, *Lanterns on the Levee*, and was thus very much a "planter" himself, he subtitled his memoir *Recollections of a Planter's Son*. In doing so he emphasized not only the importance of family and historical connections to his own sense of himself but also his feeling of inferiority to past generations. It is as if his father and the male Percys who came before him were people of great accomplishment, and he—even as a mature man—could think of himself only as their "son" and not as an equal heir to the Percy legacy. In his mind, all the best things, including Percy males, had roots in an earlier era. He self-deprecatingly refers to himself as something of a "sissy" (126).

Percy assumes the pose of southern aristocrat, keeper of the antebellum legacy, one of the last gentlemen in the midst of a civilization on the decline. In this role, he takes on a series of obligations, particularly to the region's black inhabitants. However, his idea of noblesse oblige is accompanied by an unexpected sense of himself as a victim. In a complicated way, he figures himself both as a patrician protector of the weak and as a victim of the caprices of the powerless members of the community. In a chapter of his memoir entitled "Race Relations," he argues that whites are the unmourned victims of the southern racial system:

> A superabundance of sympathy has always been expended on the Negro,
> neither undeservedly nor helpfully, but no sympathy whatever, as far
> as I am aware, has ever been expended on the white man living among
> Negroes. Yet he, too, is worthy not only of sympathy but of pity, and
> for many reasons. To live habitually as a superior among inferiors, be
> the superiority intellectual or economic, is a temptation to dishonesty
> and hubris, inevitably deteriorating. To live among a people whom,
> because of their needs, one must in common decency protect and defend
> is a sore burden in a world where one's own troubles are about all any

life can shoulder. . . . And, last, to live among a people deceptively but deeply alien and unknowable guarantees heart-aches, unjust expectations, undeserved condemnations. Yet such living is the fate of the white man in the South. He deserves all the sympathy and patience he doesn't get. (298)

Like Smith, William Alexander Percy analyzes Jim Crow in terms of its impact on white southerners. While Smith concludes that racism and segregation psychologically damaged the whites who maintained these systems of oppression, Percy argues that being forced to live among African Americans is in and of itself at times an unbearable burden. Percy's depiction of life in the segregated South stands in direct contrast to Wright's description of black suffering and victimization. To Percy, white southerners are not oppressors but instead themselves victims of a subtle kind of oppression exercised by the region's black inhabitants.

In reading *Lanterns on the Levee* for historical insights, what can we hope to extract from an account that seems so distorted in light of the historiographical literature? First of all, we must remember that the historical study of memoirs is not aimed primarily at uncovering "what actually happened" in the past. After all, it seems likely that a historian could get a better feel for what happened on Percy's plantation by studying plantation records than by reading Percy's self-interested accounts. Instead, the historical study of memoirs attempts to reveal the emotional experience of the individual actor. No one is better equipped to describe the inside of his historical moment, his thoughts and emotions about Jim Crow, than William Alexander Percy. While reading *Lanterns on the Levee*, we can hope to reconstruct empathetically Percy's felt experiences of Jim Crow. Not only are his thoughts and emotions partially constitutive of the historical reality of the time period, but his version of Jim Crow also has had an impact on the way the region is remembered. Percy is self-consciously engaged in the enterprise of influencing his readers' collective historical memory of the antebellum past as well as of Jim Crow. Although he is personally and politically motivated, we cannot conclude that his memories are pure propaganda, that he does not believe what he is saying. Percy represents his world the way he saw it, and he was blinded to data that seemed to point to a different interpretation.

Percy's memoir is primarily an account of his own life experiences, but occasionally he assumes the role of community spokesperson, a position he believes that he is both entitled to and obligated to fill as a southern aristocrat. When describing the economic situation of the Delta, he claims that "no class or individual has ever known riches. Some years the crop and prices are good and we take a trip or sport an automobile or buy another plantation; most years the crop fails or the bottom drops out of the market and we put on a new mortgage or increase the old one. Even then no one goes hungry or feels very sorry for himself" (24). This is the region as Percy wants to perceive it and the way he wants the world to see it. Although he claims to speak for the entire region with the collective "we," it soon becomes clear that he is really speaking only of southern landowners, those in the position to buy yet "another" plantation when economic times are good. By shifting from the collective "we" to the implication that he is referring only to those who already own plantations, he shows that he could not be speaking for lower class southerners. Percy may indeed have shielded himself from the fact that many poor southerners did sometimes go hungry and thus were probably due a hearty dose of self-pity. However, he could not be under the illusion that many members of these classes would ever be in the financial position to own an automobile or travel or own a piece of land of their own, let alone a plantation. This passage does not even convincingly describe Percy's own financial situation. By his own account, throughout his life, Percy had sufficient funds for education, travel, and to dole out to causes he deemed worthy. Percy may not have been rich by some standards, but for the standards of his region he stood out as prosperous indeed.

The fact that Percy claimed to speak for the entire region only to shift his commentary to refer to landowners alone is not surprising if we look at how Percy defined southern society. Percy is scornful of the poor white community, claiming that "the virus of poverty, malnutrition, and interbreeding has done its degenerative work" (20). He presents lower-class whites as in every way "inferior to the Negro." He implicates poor whites for lynchings and for excessive racial hatred while portraying his class as the protector of the African American. Scott Romine has observed that, although Percy exiles poor whites from his conception of southern community, he demonstrates an "inability to classify the Negro as an enemy."[14] Percy views patrician whites and blacks as locked into a symbiotic relationship, and he may very well mean to include the black population by association when he speaks of the southern community in collective terms.

His belief in this symbiotic relationship caused Percy to feel a profound sense of duty to the black population. He claimed, "Anybody who was anybody must feel *noblesse oblige*, must concern himself with good government, must fight, however feebly or ineffectually or hopelessly, for the public weal" (74). Because Percy felt only contempt for poor whites and thought that his own class was largely able to fend for itself, most of his charitable instincts were directed at African Americans. He viewed the black population with a complex set of emotions, feeling affection and revulsion, duty and annoyance, admiration and disgust. He was unabashed in his paternalistic racism, declaring: "I would say to the Negro: before demanding to be a white man socially and politically, learn to be a white man morally and intellectually—and to the white man: the black man is our brother, a younger brother, not an adult, not disciplined, but tragic, pitiful and loveable; act as his brother and be patient" (309).

He completes his depiction of African Americans by stating that they have "an obliterating genius for living in the present" and are "simple and affectionate people whose criminal acts do not seem to convert them into criminal characters" (23, 300). Percy's black stereotypes bear certain similarities to Smith's, demonstrating that both had internalized some of the ideas of blackness common in their culture. Smith's observation that blacks lack "ambivalence" seems to echo Percy's observation that they live in the present. Neither seems to believe that the black population can be as emotionally tortured as the white. Smith portrays blacks as lovable but with violent tendencies lurking underneath the surface. For her, razor fights represent escapism from Jim Crow realities. For Percy, who also assumes that blacks are affectionate and violent, black violence reveals their childlike nature.

It is significant that Smith and Percy draw on similar conceptual frameworks to describe the black community. They each had internalized their society's racist views about African Americans. When interacting with black people, each saw only what their racist indoctrination taught them to see. However, owing to their differing political orientations, they draw on the same stereotypes to reach different conclusions. Smith describes African Americans as long-suffering, lovable, and worthy of compassion and full inclusion into the community. Percy regards them similarly as lovable but also as inferior, in need of protection, and ill equipped for full citizenship.

Interestingly, despite his condescending descriptions of the black community, Percy demonstrates elsewhere that he closely identifies with and sometimes envies that community. McKay Jenkins has provocatively argued that "blackness for Percy . . . stands for something of which he was somehow incapable, and which somehow he was forbidden. . . . Percy's imagining of blacks as joyful innocents speaks volumes about his own tightly wound existence."[15] Percy's vision of the symbiotic relationship between whites and blacks is not just a relationship of employee and employer. He also sees upper-class whiteness and peasant blackness as a dichotomy of the intellectual and the emotive. Whites like himself are duty-bound to be the brains of the region, whereas blacks are given the more pleasurable job of expressing the emotions of the South. Percy, who views himself as stuck in the realm of duty, is envious of blacks, whom he believes dwell in the realm of feelings, who are not bound by obligation but free to enjoy life. Percy lives in terror of modernity and is afraid that the old social order and the established racial relationships are changing. He mourns, "In our brave new world a man of honor is rather like the Negro—there's no place for him to go" (72).

Needless to say, Richard Wright would not have recognized Percy's Mississippi. If we read *Black Boy* and *Lanterns of the Levee* side by side, it is not readily apparent that both authors are talking about the same historical moment and a similar geographical location. There are very few similarities in their depictions of their historical reality. Each responded to the concrete, outside reality of the same historical moment in different ways. Wright rejected the southern social order and fled from the South; Percy defended the southern way of life and devoted his life to attempting to maintain it. Each also generated a complex set of ideas and emotions in order to interpret their social world. These competing sets of ideas and feelings jointly constitute part of that reality. Furthermore, these different worldviews continue to battle each other for the way their historical moment will be interpreted and remembered in the future.

Fear of modernity is one of the overwhelming themes in *Lanterns on the Levee*. Percy strives to defend his social order and to convince his readers to embrace his version of the South, but he does so from the viewpoint that the glory days of the region are already over. The golden era of southern history is located for Percy in the antebellum past; what is left of that order is being threatened by industrialization, the mechanization of agriculture, and outside interference in southern labor and race relations. He mournfully proclaims, "Behind us a culture lies dying, before us the forces of the unknown world gather for catastrophe" (24). Percy finds that his ideas about duty and honor often conflict with the dictates of the modern world. Nowhere is the tension more acute than in his account of the Mississippi River flood of 1927.

Inhabitants of the Delta region of Mississippi were accustomed to periodic springtime floods and had installed an extensive network of levees to contain the Mississippi. However, the flood of 1927 defeated those structures and inundated the region. In April of that year, the Mississippi began to overflow its banks and then to break levees throughout Mississippi, Arkansas, and Louisiana. The citizens of the region desperately tried to contain the river, reinforcing the levees with sandbags. It was to no avail; the river flooded 27,000 square miles, displacing 700,000 people from their homes. Many towns were covered in ten feet of water.[16] When it became clear that the floodwaters would reach Greenville, the town mayor appointed Percy chairman of the local Flood Relief Committee as well as of the local Red Cross.

Percy's first order of business in his new position was to see to the evacuation of the town's white inhabitants who had not been able to leave in advance of the waters. Many were stranded on the second stories of houses, on trees, or on rooftops. Percy rounded up as many boats as he could and (with the help of local bootleggers and their motorboats) managed to safely evacuate Greenville's white citizenry. His attention then turned to the black population. According to Percy, "There were seventy-five hundred of them. . . . They were clammy and hungry, finding shelter anywhere, sleeping on any floor, piled pell-mell in oil mills or squatting miserably on the windy levee" (256).

The dilemma Percy faced was whether to evacuate the black population just as he had done with the whites or to set up a camp for them on the only bit of dry ground in the town, which was on top of the levee. Fearful of disease and concerned about the well-being of the people put under his care, Percy decided to evacuate them. However, many local planters raised strong objections to the relocation of their labor supply. They were afraid that once their tenants, sharecroppers, domestic servants, and wage laborers left the area they would not return. Percy, however, remained firm. He recalls, "I insisted I would not be bullied by a few blockhead planters into doing something I knew to be wrong—they were thinking of their pocket-books: I of the Negroes' welfare" (257). Holding firmly to his position, Percy arranged for boats to come and assist with the evacuation.

However, Percy's father, the indomitable former senator, suggested that Percy carefully weigh his decision and bring the matter before the local relief committee once again. Percy took his father's advice, holding a meeting a few days later. Much to his surprise, Percy watched as the committee members one by one recanted their former position, stating that the blacks must remain. Stunned, Percy remembers, "I argued for two hours but could not budge them. At the end of the conference, weak, voiceless, and on the verge of collapse, I told the outraged captains that their steamers must return empty" (258).

After his father's death, Percy learned that the senator had secretly canvassed behind his son's back, lobbying the committee members to change their position and to jointly conspire to keep the town's labor supply trapped on top of the levee until the floodwaters receded. Justifying his father's self-interested and treacherous behavior, Percy claimed, "He knew that the dispersal of our labor was a longer evil than the Delta flood" (258). Just as young Lillian Smith told herself that her parents were right to send young Janie away, the adult William Alexander Percy crafted a story to justify his father's behavior. He even purported to believe it. However, his avowal that losing labor was a "longer evil" pales in comparison with his earlier stated outrage at the committee's change of heart. The decision to keep local blacks in the town when evacuation would have provided them with improved sanitary conditions, better accommodations, and higher morale violated Percy's profound sense of noblesse oblige. Not only was he unable to act in what he believed was the best interest of the black community, but he was also faced with the realization that when push came to shove, his own father was far more self-interested than benevolent. This realization violated Will Percy's inflated sense of the nobility of the Percy family. If Percy had allowed himself to dwell on it, the impact would have certainly been more devastating.

Percy chose to ignore the disconnect between ideals of southern paternalism and the unjust treatment of the town's African American community. It was the only thing he could do to keep his sense of himself and his place in the community intact. Unable to assist local blacks, he turned his wrath against them instead, despairing at the manner in which they responded to their captivity. Even though Percy felt uneasy about the decision not to evacuate local blacks, he found himself unable to understand their collective dissatisfaction over conditions in the Red Cross camps. He maintained, "They had no capacity to plan for their own welfare; planning for them was another of our burdens" (258). He expected easy acquiescence to his mandates, even if he was uncomfortable with them himself.

Percy's description of life in the levee camps is at odds with the historical evidence on the subject. The historical study of *Lanterns on the Levee* demonstrates that Percy was blinded by his own class sensibilities as well as his guilt over having failed in his mission to serve as protector of the black inhabitants. According to Percy, "the Negroes had behaved admirably during the first few weeks of the flood. The camp life on the levee suited their temperaments. There was nothing for them to do except unload their rations when the boat docked. The weather was hot and pleasant. Conditions favored conversation. They worked a little, talked a great deal, and ate heartily of food which someone else paid for, and talked at night" (264). However, this situation soon changed, and it changed inexplicably from the perspective of Will Percy. The black inhabitants of the Red Cross camp soon began refusing to unload the supply boat when it arrived in camp. As a result, local police rounded up several men, forcing them to unload the boat at gunpoint. In the process, one man refused and was shot by local police, causing an uproar in the black community. Percy called a gathering at a local church, scolding the people assembled there for the man's death, claiming, "For four months I have struggled and worried and done without sleep in order to help you Negroes. Every white man in town has done the same thing. . . . Because of your sinful, shameful laziness . . . one of your own race has been killed" (267–68). Despite his harsh condemnation, Percy was able to convince only four black men to unload the boat. He describes the volunteers as "a friend of [his], a one-armed man, and two preachers who had been slaves on the Percy Place and were too old to lift a bucket" (268).

Feeling bewildered and betrayed, Percy could not understand the actions of the black community. Several weeks after this confrontation in the church, he resigned his position as head of the local relief effort, sailing the next day to Japan on vacation. He could not reconcile the gap between his conception of noblesse oblige and his having failed the black community. He also could not accept the fact that local African Americans did not seem to view him as their protector and defender. They did not even seem to believe that his intentions are good.

Percy finally concluded that the African Americans refused to unload the boat and showed other signs of resentment because of stories they read in the black newspaper, the *Chicago Defender*, which had criticized the relief effort. Percy claimed that "the Negroes at home read their Northern newspapers trustingly and believed them far more piously than the evidence before their own eyes" (264). It was inconceivable to Percy that local blacks might feel abused or betrayed by his decision not to evacuate them or that they might have legitimate complaints against the conditions in the camps. He also could not conceive of the possibility that they were able to organize a local protest. Instead he feebly concluded that they were responding to stories originating in the North.

Two reports issued by the Colored Advisory Commission give glimpses into the black perspective of the conditions at the Red Cross camps during the 1927 flood. The reports were authored by Robert Moton, Booker T. Washington's heir at Tuskegee. Moton was appointed by Herbert Hoover, chairman of the federal relief efforts. Much as Washington had done before him, Moton sought to stay in the good graces of powerful, white politicians. If anything, his reports minimize the poor conditions at the Red Cross camps. Nonetheless, Moton notes a number of shortcomings in the camps set up for the flood refugees. The most egregious violations of Red Cross policies concerned the distribution of food and other supplies. Moton claims that in several instances local whites controlled the distribution of supplies. Sometimes African Americans were charged for Red Cross foodstuffs or made to work for them. In addition, they were not automatically issued supplies. Instead they had to apply to local landowners and ask for them, giving the landowners the power to stipulate conditions on which the goods would be issued.[17]

Thus, the black men whom Percy confronted in the church, labeling them as lazy and as having been duped by the northern press, were likely engaged in a legitimate protest against the unjust way in which the Red Cross supplies were being distributed. Percy's and Moton's account of the same historical moment are completely contrary. The historiographical consensus, however, is on the side of the African Americans. The extent to which Percy was responsible for the abuses in the system is less clear. Bertram Wyatt-Brown argues that Percy knew, and disapproved of, the fact that some white landowners were controlling the distribution of Red Cross supplies. However, many of the criticisms printed against Percy in the *Chicago Defender* (such as the allegation that he withheld supplies from families without a male head of household) were untrue and unjustly damaged his reputation.[18]

This impasse between Percy and the African American community reveals the chronic lack of trust between the white and black communities. It also demonstrates the extent to which internal emotions and thoughts can influence one's perception of a historical moment. It is clear that Percy's inside experience of the Mississippi River flood of 1927 bore little resemblance to the event as interpreted by Robert Moton or any number of the African Americans in the Greenville Red Cross Camps.

Percy demonstrates a dim awareness that he does not understand the inner workings of black people nearly as well as he purports to elsewhere. Early in the text, Percy describes one of his early teachers, a redhead, who he claims had the temperament commonly associated with this hair color. In that context, he offhandedly remarks on the "Negro's interior," stating, "I am told there is no relation between what you see of him and what there is of him" (84). However, this is not an observation that Percy takes much to heart. He seems content throughout most of the text to make generalizations about black behavior and then to appear injured or confused when his assumptions are not borne out. Percy's racial ideology is so controlling that it persists even when the facts do not support his beliefs.

Like his fellow Mississippian Richard Wright, Percy gives the student of history an important glimpse at the ironic structure of the southern social world. In one memorable passage of *Lanterns on the Levee*, Percy recalls hearing blacks on his plantation performing irony. However, he initially does not understand their true meanings. Ford, his black servant, likely acting out of intermingled pity and malice, explains the exchange to him. Percy uses his literary skills to describe powerfully his initiation into an understanding of southern irony. He does so at his own expense, since he turns out to be the butt of the joke, the unsophisticated dupe who is unable to grasp the utterer's true meaning.

> In late autumn we drove to the plantation on settlement day. Cotton
> had been picked and ginned, what cash had been earned from the crop
> was to be distributed. The managers and bookkeepers had been hard at

work preparing a statement of each tenant's account for the whole year. As the tenant's name was called, he entered the office and was paid off. The Negroes filled the store and overflowed onto the porch confabulating. As we drove up, one of them asked: "Whose car is dat?" Another answered: "Dat's *us* car." I thought it was curious they didn't recognize my car, but dismissed the suspicion and dwelt on the thought of how sweet it was to have a relation between landlord and tenant so close and affectionate that to them my car was their car. Warm inside I passed through the crowd, glowing and bowing, the lord of the manor among his faithful retainers. . . . As we drove off I said:

"Did you hear what that man said?"

Ford assented, but grumpily.

"It was funny," I continued.

"Funnier than you think," observed Ford sardonically.

I didn't understand and said so.

Ford elucidated: "He meant that's the car *you* has bought with *us* money. They all knew what he meant, but you didn't and they knew you didn't. They wuz laughing to theyselves." (291)

Instead of absorbing the lesson of southern irony and realizing what a gulf exists between his understanding and experiences of the historical reality of Jim Crow and those of the laborers, Percy reacts by feeling injured and betrayed. By the standard of the time, Percy was a good landlord. He did not manipulate the books to cheat his tenants and sharecroppers at harvest time or overcharge his tenants at the plantation commissary. He helped many of them buy land. He also spoke out against lynching and police brutality.[19] As his nephew, Walker Percy, observed, such behavior branded him as a "nigger lover" in the eyes of his white contemporaries.[20]

Percy craved respect for his paternalistic virtue and was deeply hurt when it was not forthcoming. He was so imprisoned in his own worldview that he could not understand that his tenants might have reasons to resent even a good landlord. As Bertram Wyatt-Brown explained, "Well meaning as Will's philanthropy was, it could not replace genuine independence."[21] A historical study of *Lanterns on the Levee* reveals not only Percy's felt experience of the past but also the extent to which he was incapable of imagining another way that Jim Crow could be experienced. Early on in the text, Percy recalls that as a child he once told a priest that he was unfit to take communion. The priest had little time for his childish sense of piety and gave him communion anyway. Percy remembers, "It never crossed my mind I wasn't right. It never does" (88).

Percy lived his life professing this same kind of certainty. Although his autobiography reveals moments of doubt or hesitation, he quickly rids himself of any second thoughts and lets his notions of honor and southern tradition guide him. As we saw, for Lillian Smith doors occasionally open that allow one to gain some perspective and to question the structure of the social world. However, when these doors begin to swing open in Percy's mind, he quickly slams them shut.

Because Percy conceives of himself as a champion of the black underclass while the black community often seems reluctant to afford himself that status, he thinks of himself as underappreciated and misunderstood. Such feelings lead him to the conclusion that southern whites deserve sympathy. He describes himself as a champion of the weak who is himself often at the mercy of the people whom he is championing. When describing his relationship with his servant Ford, he confesses, "In the South every white man worth calling white or a man is owned by some Negro, whom he thinks he owns. . . . Ford is mine" (287). Emotionally at least, Percy does seem to be at Ford's mercy.[22]

One day Ford strolls into the bathroom while Percy is taking a shower and nonchalantly remarks, "You ain't nothing but a little old fat man. . . . Jest look at your stummick" (287). Flabbergasted that Ford is not showing him the kind of deference he expects and humiliated by the revelation that Ford perceives him as merely a middle-aged man rather than as the benign lord of the manor he fancies himself, Percy fires Ford. However, their relationship does not end there. Percy sends Ford to school for mechanics in Chicago and afterward continues to accept his long-distance phone calls asking for money. Percy does so because he persists in believing—quite accurately—that "Ford is [his] fate" (296).

Talking of Another World

WILLIE MORRIS's observation that his Mississippi was not the same place inhabited by black civil rights workers or, by extension, by his white neighbors from various political and socioeconomic backgrounds is at the heart of this analysis of literary autobiography. After reading the six memoirs under consideration here, the student of history quickly sees that there is no singular Jim Crow experience but that historical reality is inextricably intertwined with the perspectives of each individual who inhabited that world. Thus it becomes clear that sweeping historical narratives that claim to tell a history that is true for everyone may very well get the names and dates right but they gloss over the complexity of individualized and often contrary responses to a social world.

The idea that individual experiences complicate attempts at grand narration is one with which most historians agree. However, owing in part to established convention, historical writing does not always accurately capture nuanced perspectives of the past, sometimes losing track of individuals altogether, expediently transforming them into historical "types." The harried historian who is charged with the onerous task of translating a chaotic past into a coherent, written representation of that moment must often resort to speaking in terms of, for example, the "black community" or of "white reactionaries" or of "women," thereby losing some of the particularized texture of the past.

Of all the historians who have endeavored to recapture the felt experience of Jim Crow, Leon Litwack has perhaps been the most successful. In his masterful work *Trouble in Mind: Black Southerners in the Age of Jim Crow*, Litwack uses a wide variety of source materials and interjects numerous particular voices to movingly convey the multiperspectival nature of the time period. He declares his intention to capture the "interior life" of the black community, but it might be more accurate to say that he captures multiple interior "lives," numerous facets of what it meant to be black in the segregated South.[1] He uses proper names and personalized accounts as he movingly describes, for example, different forms of African American cultural expression and ways that individuals and groups resisted white oppression.

As successful as Litwack is at giving his readers a sense of how Jim Crow was felt and interpreted by black southerners from various backgrounds, there are, it seems, certain limitations to this snapshot approach. Historians rarely analyze entire texts, instead culling from larger sources and collecting bits and pieces of historical evidence. They then utilize these components to assemble their particular reconstruction of a past moment. This approach, of course, does not necessarily mean that the historian is unfamiliar with entire larger texts—in terms of structure and style as well as historical context—but oftentimes this is indeed the case.

Richard Wright's *Black Boy*, for example, is quoted widely in histories of segregation, but the complexity of Wright's experience simply cannot be captured in one carefully selected passage that has been stripped from the larger text. Remember, for example, the way young Wright learned to embrace southern irony, to say one thing and mean another, in order to survive in segregated Mississippi. Were a historian to quote a passage either before or after Wright learned this vital and complicated lesson, she or he would enshrine only one moment in Wright's evolution as representative. Litwack, for example, tells us that Wright could not "submit totally to the demands made of him," that he resented being forced to hang his head, to tell white interlocutors what they wanted to hear.[2] This is, in part, true, but to understand the complexity of Wright's evolving experiences, we must see that he finally did learn to stifle his true nature, to say one thing and mean another. His survival depended on it. Wright's awakening to Jim Crow realities was a process that cannot be captured without analyzing the text as a whole. When autobiographies are parsed and dissected to provide factual evidence or to illustrate a particular point, part of their meaning is invariably lost in the process.

Jacquelyn Dowd Hall has railed against "unspoken hierarchies" that dictate that "historical sense overrules poetic sense . . . [and that] master narratives override local knowledge."[3] An expansive understanding of the enterprise of historical writing, such as the one advocated by Hall, must challenge the idea that what constitutes historical knowledge and, by extension, historical methodology is fixed and ontologically independent, rather than being in and of itself a product of historical processes.

Much as the New Historicist literary critics have made a concerted effort to draw on some tricks from the historian's playbook by grounding their work in a historical context, historians would be well served if they similarly transgressed disciplinary boundaries. Students of history would do well to learn the lesson from their colleagues working in literature that autobiographical texts should be analyzed in their entirety. In so doing, historians would necessarily be forced to pay close attention to issues of style in addition to what a traditionalist historian might view as "substance," thereby placing poetics on par with historical sense as it has been enshrined by the discipline. Furthermore, by analyzing autobiographies in their entirety, we would displace the historian's recurrent inclination to favor master narratives over individual voices.

Indeed, in the case of literary autobiography, texts must be viewed as complete entities so that we can capture the author's full range, to see how her or his impressions, memories, and evaluations morph and change. It is this kind of complexity that is the most difficult to capture in conventional narrative histories, which invariably are rooted in a higher degree of factual certainty than exists in real life. When historians are trying to establish a sequence of events or explain causation, they must maintain a higher degree of certainty than is ever available in lived experience—for if a historian is to argue that "Event B" is a direct outgrowth of "Cause A," she or he must maintain a high degree of certitude about what "Cause A" actually entailed. An examination of literary memoirs, which are able to capture the ambivalence and confusion that are often an inherent part of felt experience, cannot fail but to unravel much of the historian's predilection toward certainty.

When analyzing Jim Crow memoirs, not only should historians consider applicable texts in their entirety, but they must also be conscientious not to impose preferred historical interpretations on a past that existed oblivious to and outside the purview of current trends in historiography. Throughout most of American history, black voices have been marginalized in attempts to write the history of the nation's past. However, in recent years, within the historical profession, the trend has been reversed. As sensitive scholars—inspired by new developments in social history from the 1970s onward—have sought to rectify earlier racist interpretations that did not inscribe full humanity toward African Americans, voices like Richard Wright's have become predominant. In fact, most current historiographical assessments of life under Jim Crow bear a certain resemblance to Wright's interpretation. Racism remains the dominant issue, and racial boundaries tend to be much more fixed than fluid. Although many historians have attempted to create depictions of a rich, black culture—much as Hurston and Gates attempt to do—totalizing racial oppression is still the predominant theme. Because institutionalized racism is the defining characteristic of the era, there is nothing disingenuous about the emphasis. However, the fact remains that in memoirs of that period racism does not always predominate in the recollection of either black or white southerners.

Clearly, ambivalent voices are missing from our new certitude that blacks fighting against oppression should be at the center of every historical narrative regarding the Jim Crow South. We do not see enough accounting for the experiences of people like Morris and Hurston and Gates who struggled as they attempted to negotiate between their political sensibilities and their sentimental attachment to a time and place. They reveal that felt experience cannot be reduced to political, economic, gender, or racial classifications. As Hall tells us, we need to develop a historical understanding that is not reductive, one that contains "both poetics and politics."[4] Sometimes when writing history, we are quick to impose prosaic structures on layered and complex social realities that are more closely akin to poetry than to prose.

The fact remains that most accounts of a historical moment do not contain a consistent, searing message the way *Black Boy* seems to. In fact, a close reading of southern autobiographies indicates that felt experience of Jim Crow contained a remarkably high degree of ambivalence. Zora Neale Hurston recognized that institutionalized racism was inexcusable. Undeniably, she suffered under it. However, she refused to let it dominate either her life or the pages of her autobiography. There was much in her life that she found rewarding, engaging, and good. Her entire existence was not spent grappling with the strictures imposed by white supremacy. Some readers of her autobiography, like Alice Walker, have refused to believe that her equivocations on the subject stemmed from her own experiences as much as from her white reader's expectations. However, we must also contemplate the notion that the account of her Jim Crow experience was not mediated as much by white expectations as by Hurston's own temperament and worldview. No doubt her depiction of Jim Crow is the end result of a combination of complex factors. However, we cannot argue with the fact that ambivalence abounds in the genre.

Henry Louis Gates Jr. benefited tremendously from the breakdown of racial barriers but was still nostalgic about the era of segregation. William Alexander Percy was an inveterate white supremacist who suffered when he felt devalued and misunderstood by the supposedly inferior African Americans in his community. Lillian Smith was outraged by white oppression but found it difficult to indict her family and close friends for being part of an unjust system. Similarly, Willie Morris loved and hated his native Mississippi in nearly equal proportions and, on occasion, even seemed to internalize its principles unconsciously. Thus we see that ambivalence is fundamental rather than exceptional to our analysis of felt experience of the time period. We must adjust our historical understanding of Jim Crow accordingly and avoid populating our historical landscape solely with stock characters of white villains and black martyrs, southern apologists and social critics.

Our examination of diverse memoirs from the era of segregation seeks to demonstrate that there is no fixed, singular historical reality that can reliably be understood as absolutely definitive. Furthermore, our ability to refeel a past moment is enhanced if we study autobiography in its entirety, taking into account literary style as well as reportage of historical facts. Finally, we must evolve beyond textbook understandings of felt experience, which undoubtedly oversimplify both white and black responses to Jim Crow. Ambivalence and uncertainty, rather than clarity and simplicity, characterized the felt experience of most. With these principles in mind, let us revisit the six texts considered in this book in order to paint the most comprehensive picture that we can of the time period. We will take a somewhat extended look at Wright's and Hurston's memories, in part because the contrast between the depictions in these two autobiographies is the starkest and thus the most difficult to reconcile. Furthermore, a prolific body of literary criticism has raised a number of provocative questions about the veracity of both *Black Boy* and *Dust Tracks on a Road*, which must be addressed in some fashion before reaching a conclusion.

Richard Wright and Zora Neale Hurston

For Richard Wright, Jim Crow reality was unremittingly bleak. He paints a picture of a cruel and tyrannical South, where the slightest mistake could result in deadly consequences for a person of color. He gives voice to the anger and bitterness he felt about Jim Crow racism and the devastating impact he believed the southern caste system had on the psychological health of the black community. He mobilizes the anger, dread, and fear he felt to paint this compelling and grim memoir of his childhood. Curiously, these emotions have little in common with Zora Neale Hurston's feelings about the same historical moment. Although *Dust Tracks* does reveal her profound perception of southern racism, this awareness is by no means the primary focus of her autobiography. For her, childhood in the Jim Crow South was filled with a considerably wider and more conflicting range of emotions than for Wright. Her memories are filled not only with adversity but also with adventure, not only with sorrow but also with joy. The greatest tragedy of her childhood was the death of her mother, an event far more traumatic in her personal development than any encounters with white racism. Her recollections of Jim Crow are not dominated by memories of white hostility. She deliberately places the issue of racism on the periphery of both the hardships and the triumphs she recounts.

As children, both Wright and Hurston endeavor to leave the South. For Wright, it seems, his very survival depends on such an escape. When he is preparing to leave home, he tells his sickly mother, who begs him not to leave, "I've got to go, mama. I can't live this way."[5] For Hurston as a child, the thought of leaving home is initially a pleasant, meandering daydream, a desire to see what the rest of the world is like rather than to the flee from the one she knew. As a small child she recalled sitting on the gate post in front of her home, watching white travelers going by and inquiring of them, "Don't you want me to go a piece of the way with you?"[6] Thus Hurston actively flagged down the same kind of people from whom Wright was so eager to flee. Biographical information reveals that Wright steadily moved geographically away from the Arkansas and Mississippi life he describes in *Black Boy*, moving to Memphis, then Chicago, New York, and finally Paris. Hurston, in contrast, left the South, experienced life in the black metropolis of Harlem, but returned to Florida regularly, ultimately remaining there permanently.

Some critics of both *Black Boy* and *Dust Tracks* have accused the authors of exaggerating, equivocating, or even fabricating in their memoirs. Unsurprisingly, many of Wright's readers have been astounded by what Robert Stepto describes as the "death-like chill of Wright's (albeit rhetorical) vision of Negro America."[7] Yoshinobu Hakutani summarizes the feelings of those readers who are skeptical of *Black Boy*'s veracity by saying, "They feel that the world, bad as it is, cannot be so bad as Wright says it is."[8] In his 1945 review of *Black Boy*, W. E. B. Du Bois argues that the book is "patently and terribly overdrawn."[9] Wright's harsh depiction of the black community as well as his own sense of detachment from that community runs counter to a tendency in much African American literature as well as in African American historiography to depict the black community as a bastion against the hostile, white world. Unable to recognize the world Wright describes, some critics, including Du Bois, have suggested that the book should be read as "creative writing rather than simply a record of life."[10]

Skeptics of Wright's veracity have asserted several claims to back up their positions. Timothy Dow Adams, among others, has noted that in *Black Boy* Wright frequently uses "dialogue marked with quotation marks," suggesting a high degree of fiction in the story and encouraging readers to receive the text as a novel rather than as a traditional autobiography.[11] Wright biographer Michel Fabre has identified many incidents in *Black Boy* that he regards as exaggerated or as partially deceptive. However, by and large, the allegations that Fabre and other Wright scholars have raised about the biographical accuracy of *Black Boy* generally pertain to issues of emphasis or noninclusion rather than purposeful falsification.

For example, Fabre corroborates that Wright grew up in poverty but faults Wright for failing to mention either his mother's work as a schoolteacher or the fact that her family, the Wilsons, before their financial ruin and relocation to Jackson, had once been a prominent family in Natchez.[12] Fabre suggests that Wright purposefully omits these details in order to emphasize his proletarian roots. However, it is equally plausible that, although his family had once enjoyed happier economic times, the severe hunger and poverty he experienced for so many years in Jackson and elsewhere obliterated and supplanted any more pleasant memories. Fabre also points out that, while an adolescent, Wright worked for the Walls, a benevolent white family. Wright's biographer suggests that Wright omitted this information because it would complicate his depiction of unrelenting white oppression.[13] However, the degree to which the Wall family members were indeed "liberal and generous employers" is objectively unverifiable. Moreover, it is questionable whether what may be regarded as liberal in segregated Mississippi would have been even nearly adequate enough to win the admiration of the introspective and fiercely proud Richard Wright. Most other examples of so-called discrepancies between the text and Wright's life are similarly specious and problematic. In general, a significant number of historians and biographers who have analyzed the text have embraced most of Wright's descriptions of his childhood as factual and reliable.

Zora Neale Hurston faced similar detractors of her autobiographical efforts. While many of Wright's critics focused incredulity on his harsh portrayal of the black community, some of Hurston's critics seethed over her unwillingness to contend with racism directly. After reading *Dust Tracks*, Arna Bontemps declared, "Miss Hurston deals very simply with the more serious aspects of Negro life in America—she ignores them."[14] Robert Hemenway more mildly describes *Dust Tracks* as a "discomfiting book [that] has probably harmed Hurston's reputation."[15] Other critics of *Dust Tracks* have focused on its limitations in other areas.

It is now a well-known fact that Hurston lied about her age. She shaved as much as a decade off her age not only when writing *Dust Tracks* but also throughout her life. The fact that she had been lying about her age for twenty-five years when she sat down to write her autobiography posed, as her biographer Valerie Boyd put it mildly, a "logistical problem."[16] She solves the problem by being evasive and by allowing her readers to infer what they will about her chronological age. Of course, since Hurston lied about age throughout her life, it is understandable that she would do so in her memoir as well. Her life experiences, her Jim Crow reality, were colored by the need to evade, dissemble, and fib to perpetuate her story. Her autobiography should and does reflect that even on a very rudimentary level Hurston spent her life fighting the facts and forging an identity that suited her. In *Dust Tracks* Hurston claims that she was born in the all-black town of Eatonville. However, a recently uncovered family Bible lists her birthplace as Notasulga, Alabama. Since none of the older Hurston children were born in Eatonville, Boyd speculates that Hurston may have lied about her birthplace to keep up her lie about her age. She may also have fabricated this imaginary account because of her strong desire to have been born in the all-black town of Eatonville, which she adored.

In a reassessment of *Dust Tracks* written twenty years after Robert Hemenway's pioneering literary biography of Hurston, Pam Bordelon has pointed out other ways in which Hurston's version of her life differs from autobiographical data. For example, Bordelon argues that Hurston's stepmother was not "the shrew . . . that Hurston describes in *Dust Tracks*."[17] However, such an evaluation, based solely on testimony from Hurston's niece, is similarly subjective and can hardly be used to indict Hurston's truthfulness. Bordelon also claims that Hurston's father never divorced her stepmother as Hurston claimed in *Dust Tracks*. Hurston's assertion that the divorce took place may be a misunderstanding, an example of wishful thinking, or a fabrication. However, most of the falsehoods that Bordelon points out in *Dust Tracks* are lies of omission. She claims, for example, that Hurston saw her siblings more frequently than she acknowledges and that she worked for the Works Progress Administration, despite neglecting to mention this in *Dust Tracks*. Nonetheless, Valerie Boyd contends that "Zora does not tell many (if any) out-and-out lies about her life."[18]

Therefore, it appears that many of the events recounted both in *Black Boy* and *Dust Tracks* are literally verifiable to a significant degree. Both authors declared their intention to write autobiography, and the vast majority of people, places, and events mentioned in the text are externally verifiable. Uneasiness about the textual descriptions of each of these individual perspectives has been centered on questions of emphasis and omission, and much of the criticism comes from readers who simply do not hear what they would like to hear. For some, a more palatable rendering of Jim Crow history may have been something of a combination of *Black Boy* and *Dust Tracks*, integrating Wright's indictment of racism with Hurston's celebration of black folk culture. Clearly, such a synthesis does not exist. What do we make, then, of these two very different texts as they are? And in what ways do the obviousese deliberate falsehoods, suspected exaggerations, and lies of omission diminish the value of these texts as historical resources?

We know that autobiographers (Wright and Hurston included) sometimes conceal the truth and occasionally exaggerate, either deliberately or inadvertently. After all, memories are faulty and potentially unreliable, and memories change. However, misrepresentation, conscious or otherwise, is part of historical reality. It is also part of historical memory, for these memoirists are attempting not only to describe what their past was like but also to determine how it should be remembered in the future. What Wright and Hurston do when they embellish or emphasize one aspect of their lives or their personalities at the expense of another is emblematic of what all people do. Misrepresentations, false impressions, bias, and misremembering are invariable components of human perception.

Historical reality, specifically the inside of a historical moment, can be composed of both lying and truth telling, remembering, forgetting, and perhaps reinventing. When trying to ascertain "what really happened" in a historical moment, we must attempt to construct the entire puzzle from various competing elements. However, when determining what the past felt like and looked liked from the perspective of a historical agent, we must leave these muddled elements intact and disconnected in order to accurately embody the genuine complexity of human perception.

Wright's and Hurston's obfuscations and omissions, their emphases and exaggerations reveal a great deal about themselves and their world. Perhaps the evils of Jim Crow were so overpowering for Wright that he became incapable of joy, bereft of optimism, and any sense of personal happiness was repressed deep inside his wounded soul. In contrast, perhaps Hurston felt that overemphasis on the "race problem" would eclipse her natural sense of well-being and that labeling herself a member of an oppressed race would diminish her individuality. To avoid inhibiting her potential, she lived her life and wrote a memoir to counter that tendency. Wright's and Hurston's emphases and perhaps their exaggerations may reveal what they were afraid was true (in the case of Wright) or what they wished could be so (in the case of Hurston). Their representations of the past also dictated the way they wanted themselves and the past to be remembered. Wright perceived himself as a protester and attempted to create a grim portrait of what he was fighting against. Hurston figured herself an artist and a free spirit who wanted to capture the source of her inspiration.

An examination of the personal history of these autobiographers illustrates much consistency in their backgrounds. Why, then, are their life narratives so dissimilar? After all, both are African Americans who grew up in the first half of the twentieth century in the rural segregated South. Against all odds, especially for those with similar upbringings, each became a published writer. Parallels can readily be observed in their emotional histories as well. Both enjoyed a positive relationship with their mother, yet each experienced considerable difficulties with other family members, especially their father. Each had to cope with the loss of their mother. Hurston's died when she was still a child. Wright's mother came in and out of prominence in his life because of the ravages of a debilitating illness. Both read voraciously and struggled arduously to get an education. Both worked as domestics in white homes. Then both traveled north, where they began writing careers. Furthermore, in temperament and personality they share some fundamental characteristics. They were highly intelligent, independent, outspoken, creative, yet regularly misunderstood as children. And most important, the racial realities of the Jim Crow South formed the backdrop for their childhood. However, as we have seen, these parallel experiences did not translate into similar Jim Crow autobiographies.

This observation leads us to investigate the ways in which their life experiences were essentially different. Obviously, despite considerable similarities, there are invariably innumerable differences to explore when comparing the backgrounds of any two individuals. For example, Wright grew up in Arkansas and Mississippi, Hurston in Florida. Even more significant, Hurston's early childhood was spent in the all-black town of Eatonville, where she was exposed to fewer of the cruelties of white racism than was Wright. Clearly, the two are of different genders, and Hurston was seventeen years older than Wright (although she would have claimed only seven or so of those years). They held many dissimilar political convictions and advocated significantly different theories about the artist's role in the world. As established writers, each was critical of the other's work. Wright claimed, for example, that *Their Eyes Were Watching God* was addressed to a white audience whose "chauvinistic tastes [Hurston] knows how to satisfy."[19] When reviewing *Uncle Tom's Children*, Hurston claimed that "not one act of understanding and sympathy comes to pass in the entire novel."[20] These statements may well summarize how each may have felt about the other's autobiographical efforts as well.

Do these obvious differences and personal peculiarities help explain the contrasting depictions of Jim Crow in each memoir? Unquestionably, Hurston's gender and geographical origin played a significant role in influencing her judgments and attitudes when compared with Wright's outlook. Despite these important distinctions, one could nevertheless assume that the experiences they held in common would result in a more pronounced agreement about what life was like in the southern United States in the first half of the twentieth century. After all, each attended segregated schools in segregated neighborhoods, encountered water fountains, restrooms, movie theaters, parks, and swimming pools labeled "white" or "colored," and habitually suffered the deprivations of second-class citizenship in the South. Although the black community of Eatonville had perhaps moderated some of the harshness of southern life for Hurston, she soon lost this support, moving away to attend boarding school. Furthermore, after her mother's death, Hurston drifted through the South working odd jobs, including working as a maid in the homes of white families. Throughout this period at least, Hurston must have experienced many of the hardships about which Wright wrote so earnestly. Conversely, Wright certainly must have been exposed to considerably more positive aspects of black community life than is acknowledged in his autobiography. The brief passage in the text where he recounts local folklore suggests, for example, that he must have at least heard some of the same stories and songs that meant so much to Hurston. Consequently, it seems difficult indeed to reconcile these diverse worldviews despite the common threads from which their lives are woven.

We can continue to speculate, however, that their worldviews are different because their Jim Crow experiences were filtered through their own perceptions, which were impacted by their personalities, their politics, their socioeconomic situations, and a whole host of other factors. Their Jim Crow memories were influenced, colored, even changed, not only by the people they were but also in response to the people that they had become at the time their memoirs were written. Therefore, even if the outside of the historical moments in which they participated had strikingly similar characteristics, their inward participation—the thoughts and feelings that constituted the inside of their historical realities—was strikingly and understandably different.

That being said, should we infer that even a careful and analytical reading of Richard Wright or Zora Neale Hurston provides insights only into how these distinctive individuals felt while living in the Jim Crow south? What about the countless others who participated in and created the same historical reality but who did not leave behind complex literary memoirs describing the world from their point of view? What insights can we gain about the lives of those people from the written accounts of Wright and Hurston?

To some extent, *Black Boy* is only the story of Richard Wright, his experiences, his perceptions of the social world in which he lived. The same is true, of course, for *Dust Tracks* and Zora Neale Hurston. However, we can assume that some of their thoughts, feelings, and perceptions were similar to those of other people. Conscientious readers who seek to live vicariously the experiences of Hurston and Wright must mobilize their own emotions to identify with the writer's elusive feelings and perceptions. If such a reader is successful in the search for historical insights into Wright's and Hurston's emotions and sensations today, then those individuals who actually lived through the same social reality must have empathized that much more acutely with the authors. Clearly, these literary memoirs, like all literature, are simultaneously particular and universal. They not only convey Wright's and Hurston's particular recollections of their lives but also provide universal insights about the human experience.

Hurston's Jim Crow experience complicates Wright's version, indicating that his portrayal cannot be read simply as "the Jim Crow experience." However, through his literary rendering of extreme pain and anger, Wright does indeed present insights into how Jim Crow might have been perceived and experienced from the perspective of overwhelming anger, resentment, and apprehension, emotions many of his contemporaries certainly endured. In contrast, Hurston's memoir might be read as, for example, a study of anger denied. Certainly others must have similarly preferred to deemphasize white oppression, to ignore its impact whenever possible, and to go on about the business of living. Many, no doubt, experienced Jim Crow from a combination of these perspectives. Others reacted in ways not described by either Wright or Hurston.

In her succinct and eloquent style, Hurston acknowledges the multiperspectival nature of social reality, noting, "Nothing that God ever made is the same thing to more than one person. That is natural. There is no single face in nature, because every eye that looks upon it, sees it from its own angle. So every man's spice-box seasons his own food."[21] Thus Hurston does not claim to speak for anyone beside herself when writing her Jim Crow memoir. We can assume, however, given the power of literature to universalize human experiences, that much of what she said inadvertently resonates with other people or speaks to aspects of the experiential nature of Jim Crow. Hurston's and Wright's experiences are to some extent emblematic of the collectively felt experience of Jim Crow and simultaneously only the personal experiences of the authors.

We must keep in mind that these conflicting depictions of Jim Crow are not only responses to the social world of Jim Crow but are also constitutive of it. Wright's and Hurston's contrary and sometimes contradictory thoughts and feelings about Jim Crow constitute the historical reality of the era. As established in chapter 1, historical reality is, by its nature, perspectival. Although Wright's and Hurston's Jim Crow memoirs offer significantly different accounts of the same historical time period, each should be considered authentic. We must strive to understand and experience both if we want to formulate an accurate conception of the historical reality of the period in question. Each introduces and highlights elements of which the complex whole is composed.

Lillian Smith and William Alexander Percy

Lillian Smith and William Alexander Percy consider themselves to be both chroniclers of their particular lives and historians of their region. Smith's portrayal of southern history illustrates the way in which African Americans were systematically excluded and persecuted by a calculating white population whose own psychological health and well-being were damaged in the process. Percy writes about a glorious antebellum past populated by contented slaves and benevolent, intelligent slave owners. These memoirists fervently attempt to compose the historical narrative not only of their own lives but also of the South as a whole.

Both authors are unquestionably devoted to the South. Smith regards it as congenial yet profoundly defective. Percy depicts the South as having experienced a period of significant decline from its former glory and, in addition, portrays the region as having been unfairly vilified and misunderstood. Both seek to revise the narrative of the South as a veritable cultural wasteland composed of victimized blacks and undereducated whites who perpetually incite racial violence through lynch mobs. Smith delicately argues that most whites were not racists but rather conformists. Percy figures himself and his class as enlightened aristocrats looking out for the best interests of the region's black population.

Smith and Percy characterize white southerners as victims, a description that is not typically represented in the historiography of the era. Smith claims that white southerners were deeply wounded by a debilitating system of racism that her generation inherited but did not create. Her analysis becomes especially surprising when she claims that whites were as victimized by Jim Crow as were blacks. In this regard, her personal assessment and recollections run contrary to nearly all valued historical data. Ultimately, black southerners were indubitably on the losing end of Jim Crow inequalities regardless of how one quantifies these disparities—socially, economically, emotionally, or politically. However, as a memoirist writing from the province of recollection and without any generic obligation to social scientific facts, Smith's observations not only make perfect sense but are also historically revealing. Despite her heroism and remarkably good intentions, she was, like many, fundamentally unable to imagine empathetically her way into another person's subject position. Therefore, it was her suffering and the torment of her friends and family that were at the center of her observations, indelibly coloring her analysis of segregation.

William Alexander Percy further advances this assessment with his more extreme assertion that upper-class whites like himself were the victims of an ungrateful and unrefined black population. In a peculiar way, he feels burdened by the system of segregation, not because he thinks the system is immoral, not because he is willing to ascribe full humanity to the black population, but because he resents his feeling of responsibility for the well-being of the black population. He views African Americans as ungrateful children, unaware or unconcerned about the dreadful responsibilities that he believes must accompany white privilege.

Neither Smith nor Percy was the first to observe that racism took its toll on the perpetrators, not just on the victims of the ideology. The towering figure Frederick Douglass made a similar observation in the nineteenth century. However, Smith's and Percy's analysis of Jim Crow is contrary to contemporary historical interpretation because these authors place the subjective white experience at the heart of Jim Crow, neither making apologies for their privileged subject position nor acknowledging these psychological injuries as secondary to the affliction of the black community. Perhaps this perception can be anticipated in the case of William Alexander Percy. After all, he is indeed an advocate for white supremacy. It is, however, somewhat perplexing that Lillian Smith, an outspoken proponent of integration, did not make greater efforts to decenter her own perceptions. However, Smith is impervious to the orthodoxies of the present, and, although tempting, it is problematic to view her analysis of Jim Crow from our current vantage point. Her memoir reveals her notable ability to challenge the framework of her social world while it inadvertently also reveals that she was very much a product of her time.

In addition to placing whites at the center of their analysis, both Smith and Percy embrace stereotypical ideas about blackness, viewing people of color as somehow childlike, simpleminded, and violent. Their similar descriptions reveal how deeply embedded each was in the ideology of their region. Clearly, each had imbibed hearty doses of the prescribed worldview. Intriguingly each drew on the same ideological currents to draw radically different moral and political conclusions. Reading Smith and Percy side by side, we see that neither fits neatly into the mold of reactionary or of radical social critic. In fact, like Wright and Hurston, Percy and Smith share much in common even as they deliberately position themselves on opposite ends of the political spectrum.

A comparison of these two memoirs illustrates that white conceptions of Jim Crow reality were intermittently dissimilar, contradictory, and conflicting and simultaneously related, comparable, and similar. Whereas Smith saw herself and other southern whites as both victims and perpetrators, Percy claimed the amalgamated status of both protector and victim of the African American population. Confusion, uncertainty, and multiplicity dominate both *Killers of the Dream* and *Lanterns on the Levee*, revealing that these white memoirists were not any more at peace with the Jim Crow system than was Wright or Hurston.

Once again we see that there is no distinct comprehensive Jim Crow experience, either from a white or black perspective. The composite experiences of each participant are far too convoluted, too conflicted, and too ambivalent to allow for a singularly accurate, all-encompassing description. Even William Alexander Percy, a southern aristocrat, cannot fill the archetypal role of racist southern planter. *Lanterns on the Levee* reveals ambivalences lurking behind his racial ideology. The extent to which he is genuinely hurt by the behavior of the black people whom he deems as inferior is baffling and complicated and should be regarded as the substance of real life rather than of historical fiction.

Henry Louis Gates Jr. and Willie Morris

While Willie Morris was at Oxford studying under a Rhodes fellowship, he concluded a paper on the English Reform Act of 1832 by stating, "Just how close the people of England came to a revolution in 1832 is a question that we shall leave with the historians." His tutor responded to Morris's rather inconclusive analysis by remarking, "But Morris, we *are* the historians."[22] That admonition fueled him as he wrote *North Toward Home*, no doubt inspiring him in his scrupulous honesty in describing, among other things, his unthinkingly cruel racist behavior as a child. Gates, too, as he sat down to write *Colored People*, saw himself as engaged in an intellectual enterprise, not only documenting the particulars of his own life but also writing his way into a distinct literary tradition.

Both men were artful and reflective memoirists whose comparable journeys began in small, southern towns. Later in life, each became an esteemed, northern public intellectual. Despite their different racial identifications, each describes his life with surprising similarity. According to conventional wisdom, any pragmatic depiction of this historical period should illustrate the bleak and gloomy nature of their time and place. However, both chronicle positive childhood experiences and appear remarkably sentimental about their early lives. Yet there is an unmistakable tension surrounding these nostalgic memories, as if each man intuitively acknowledges he should *know better*. Writing in 1967, just after the close of the nonviolent phase of the civil rights movement, Willie Morris realizes that in order to uphold his liberal status he must emotionally disassociate from the Mississippi of his childhood. He was tormented by the media coverage of civil rights activities and of urban rioting, remarking, "[The images] remained with me not in righteousness, but in simple horror; they obsessed me not merely on their own terms, but out of agonies I had seen in my own past . . . these images were part of me; I could not say I was innocent of them."[23] Part of his revulsion derives from the nature of the specific events, but much of his emotional reaction stems from his inability to reconcile these appalling episodes with his idyllic childhood memories.

Like Morris, Henry Louis Gates Jr., when his memoir was written, had become a public intellectual and achieved remarkable success at the highest levels of academia. By this time, Gates, in all probability, must have felt like the quintessential poster child for integration. On a different level, however, he also felt nostalgic for the sense of intimacy and familiarity that the black community lost after the era of segregation. The institutionalized racism of Jim Crow cannot be but anathema to grown-up Gates. However, several of the by-products of that iniquitous system were undeniably appealing. Therefore, like Morris, the reconciliation of his genuine memories of life under Jim Crow with his intellectually mature understanding of what those recollections should entail was indeed difficult to achieve.

Perhaps having written their autobiographies during or even after the civil rights movement, Gates and Morris were somewhat more optimistic and could justifiably afford a sense of nostalgia that the authors who wrote while living within the depths of Jim Crow could not. Or perhaps it is equally plausible that the conflicted emotions, the ambivalence, the dubious struggle between the impulses of the mind and those of the heart experienced by these later writers are indeed characteristic of more contemporary memoirs as well.

In order to achieve a more comprehensive understanding of Jim Crow, we should aspire to experience vicariously the sensations, perceptions, and impressions of these authors and the many others who have willingly exposed their consciousness and souls to our examination. From Richard Wright we experience a sense of anger, resentment, and fear. Zora Neale Hurston expresses both joy and ambivalence. Henry Louis Gates Jr. shows a feeling of nostalgia, while Willie Morris demonstrates both feelings of guilt and a bond to his childhood home. Similarly, Lillian Smith loves the region of her birth yet simultaneously abhors its history of racism, and even William Alexander Percy experiences feelings of power and responsibility combined with those of weakness and despair. The result is an exceedingly multifaceted and complicated portrait of the era, one that fundamentally defies easy generalizations and simplifications.

If we consider historical reality to be composed of an intricate collage of myriad individual experiences in which each distinct episode contains a lifetime of thoughts and emotions, actions and reactions, we acquire a more profound understanding of a particular period. A historical endeavor of this nature requires dynamically active and emotive inquiry, as well as an appreciation of the historical moment from a variety of viewpoints and perspectives. And unmistakably, this methodology allows for few unambiguous resolutions to historical challenges.

Therefore, we should embrace the full implications of Morris's realization that his Mississippi was a different place than that of the SNCC worker. Moreover, we see additional competing versions of Mississippi if we compare the birthplaces of Wright and Percy. Wright surely would have denigrated Percy's depiction of himself as a victim of Jim Crow, much as Percy would have had little appreciation for Wright's account of growing up black in Mississippi. In fact, Percy proclaimed that in the Delta "no one goes hungry or cold or feels very sorry for himself"; Wright—who grew up in a number of towns in or near the Mississippi Delta—describes hunger as a constant companion.[24] Neither would have recognized the state as the other person had described it. They would have been baffled at each other's descriptions. A thorough reading of *Black Boy* reveals a southern landscape permeated with terror and foreboding. For Percy, the Mississippi countryside was filled with bittersweet nostalgic recollections. These divergent descriptions are simultaneously contradictory and true. The Mississippi where Wright grew up offered a reality fundamentally separate from that presented to Percy. The Mississippi countryside contains no independent meaning other that the one imposed on it by the individuals who examine it, interact with it, live it, and remember it.

Each depiction of the South contains part of the social reality of Jim Crow, and we should endeavor to understand all of these depictions. There is no all-encompassing perspective from which we can identify *the* Mississippi—or, by extension, *the* South. The social and emotional reality of Jim Crow exists solely from the standpoint of the historical agents who created and sustained it, and an understanding of this reality is unattainable without recognizing their distinct individual perspectives. The inspired literary memoirists we have considered all utilized their ingenuity and imagination to capture the universe as it existed from their point of view. Examined concurrently, they provide a richly valuable and elaborately layered description of the Jim Crow experience that cannot be captured by broad, historiographical overviews but that offers a reality that must be felt to be genuinely understood.

NOTES

INTRODUCTION

1. In the 1990s several literary critics began experimenting with "personal criticism," inserting their own life experiences into their scholarly work. For a brief discussion of criticism by scholars "going public as private subjects," see Miller, "But Enough about Me."

2. Stanford, *Introduction to the Philosophy of History*, 55.

3. Quoted in Prins, "Oral History," 114.

4. Inscoe, "Black, White, and Southern."

5. Olney, *Studies in Autobiography*, xiv–xv.

6. Leibowitz, *Fabricating Lives*, xvii.

7. Billson, "Memoir," 263.

8. Popkin, *History, Historians, and Autobiography*, 15.

9. Gusdorf, "Conditions and Limits of Autobiography," 38.

10. Sayre, "Proper Study," 241.

11. Eakin, *Touching the World*, 143.

12. For example, see Kadar, *Essays on Life Writing*; De Man, "Autobiography as Defacement"; and Bruss, *Autobiographical Acts*.

13. Lejeune, *On Autobiography*, 4.

14. In describing the "intentional fallacy," W. M. Wimsatt emphatically states that the "design or intention of the author is neither available nor desirable as a standard for judging the success of a work of literary art." See Wimsatt, *Verbal Icon*, 3.

15. Livingston, "Intentionalism in Aesthetics," 835.

16. Levinson, "Intention and Interpretation," 222.

17. Popkin, *History, Historians, and Autobiography*, 31.

18. For more information about minstrelsy, see Mahan, *Behind the Burnt Cork Mask*.

19. Stearns and Lewis, *Emotional History of the United States*, 1.

ONE. SUBJECTIVITY AND THE FELT EXPERIENCE OF HISTORY

1. Quoted in Thompson, *Voice of the Past*, 104.

2. Popkin, "Historians on the Autobiographical Frontier," 726. Popkin is quoting from Clark, *Critical Historian*, 67.

3. Acton letter reprinted in Stern, *Varieties of History*, 249.

4. Nagel, *View from Nowhere*, 7.

5. Stanford, *Introduction to the Philosophy of History*, 56.

6. Popkin, "Historians on the Autobiographical Frontier," 727.

7. Du Bois, *Black Reconstruction in America*, 1.

8. Stanford, *Introduction to the Philosophy of History*, 55.

9. Novick, *That Noble Dream*, 2.

10. Elton, *Return to Essentials*, 27, 34, 41, 43, 49.

11. Windschuttle, *Killing of History*.

12. Ibid., 36.

13. Eakin, *Touching the World*, 143.

14. Barthes, *Roland Barthes*, 56.

15. Quoted in Megill, "Reception of Foucault by Historians," 117.

16. Foucault, "Nietzsche, Genealogy, History," 158.

17. Shiner, "Reading Foucault," 387. See Foucault, "Nietzsche, Genealogy, History," 139–64.

18. Confino, "Some Random Thoughts," 37.

19. Ibid., 34.

20. Eakin, *Touching the World*, 54.

21. Ibid., 23.

22. Nowell-Smith, "Constructionist Theory of History," 5.

23. Lorenz, "Historical Knowledge and Historical Reality," 298.

24. Ibid., 327.

25. Putnam, *Reason, Truth, and History*, 49–50.

26. Lorenz, "Historical Knowledge and Historical Reality," 312.

27. Ibid., 313.

28. Putnam, *Reason, Truth, and History*, 49–50.

29. Appleby, Hunt, and Jacob, *Telling the Truth about History*, 247.

30. Ibid., 250.

31. Anchor, "Realism and Ideology," 109.

32. Ibid., 119.

33. Dilthey, *Pattern and Meaning in History*, 89.

34. Ibid., 85.

35. Collingwood, *Idea of History*.

36. Ibid., 214.

37. Ibid., 215.

38. Stanford, *Introduction to the Philosophy of History*, 72.

39. Dilthey, *Pattern and Meaning in History*, 67.

40. Stearns and Lewis, introduction to *Emotional History of the United States*, 1.

41. Barzun and Graff, *Modern Researcher*, 40.

42. Ibid.

43. Brian Attebery, "American Studies," 324.

44. Stockley, "Empathetic Reconstruction," 58.

45. Wolff, "Narrative Time," 216.
46. Berger and Luckmann, *Social Construction of Reality*.
47. Collin, *Social Reality*, 2–3.
48. Wolff, "Narrative Time," 214.
49. Ibid., 220.
50. Ibid., 219.
51. Ibid., 221.
52. Quoted in Canary and Kozicki, *Writing of History*, 42.
53. Thompson, *Voice of the Past*, 135.
54. White, "Telling More," 14, 15.
55. Adams, *Telling Lies*, x.
56. Nora, "Between Memory and History," 8.
57. Ibid., 8–9.
58. Ibid., 14.
59. Ibid., 15.
60. Thelan, "Memory and American History," 1121.
61. Crews, *Childhood*, 1.
62. Thompson, *Voice of the Past*, 139.
63. Thelan, "Memory and American History," 1119.
64. Blight, "W. E. B. Du Bois," 46.
65. Fields, "What One Cannot Remember Mistakenly," 153.
66. Kundera, *Book of Laughter and Forgetting*, 3.
67. Said, "Invention, Memory, Place," 176.

TWO. LITERARY TECHNIQUES AND HISTORICAL UNDERSTANDING

1. Egan, *Mirror Talk*, 30.
2. Eagleton, *Literary Theory*, 4.
3. Iacocca and Novak, *Lee Iacocca*, 3.
4. Nabokov, *Speak, Memory*, 19.
5. Popkin, *History, Historians, and Autobiography*, 49.
6. Eagleton, *Literary Theory*, 4.
7. Blight, "W. E. B. Du Bois," 53.
8. Ibid., 55.
9. O'Meally, "On Burke and the Vernacular," 245.
10. Franke, "Metaphor and the Making of Sense," 147.
11. Gibbs, "When Is Metaphor?" 595.
12. Shen, "Cognitive Aspects of Metaphor Comprehension," 568–69.
13. Gibbs, "When Is Metaphor?" 597.
14. Anchor, "Realism and Ideology," 116.
15. Wright, *Black Boy (American Hunger)*, 384.
16. Briggs, *This Dark World*, 76.

17. Wolff, *Moneybags Must Be So Lucky*, 32–35.

18. Morris, *North Toward Home*, 399–400.

19. Hirsch, "Transhistorical Intentions," 552.

20. Clifford, "On Ethnographic Allegory," 100.

21. Ibid., 99.

22. Hirsch, "Transhistorical Intentions," 553.

23. Anchor, "Realism and Ideology," 115.

24. Harlan, "Intellectual History," 589. Harlan is paraphrasing some of the thought of J. G. A. Pocock.

25. Pocock, *Virtue, Commerce, and History*, 10.

26. Smith, *Killers of the Dream*, 129, 117.

27. Welty, "Place in Fiction," 62.

28. Howarth, "Writing Upside Down," 4–5.

29. Percy, *Lanterns on the Levee*, 156.

30. Berry, "Class Southerner," 167.

31. Ibid., 169.

32. Smith, *Killers of the Dream*, 87.

THREE. AFRICAN AMERICAN MEMOIRISTS REMEMBER JIM CROW

1. Wright's first draft of his autobiography was titled *American Hunger* and chronicled his childhood years, his migration to Chicago, his involvement with the Communist Party, and his early attempts to become a writer. In 1945, only the first part of the book, dealing with his childhood in the South, was published under the title *Black Boy*. A restored version of the text as Wright intended was published in 1991 by the Library of America under the title *Richard Wright: Later Works*. In this book, I am quoting from a restored edition, but my analysis concerns the first half of the book, which describes his life in the Jim Crow South.

2. Hurston, *Dust Tracks on a Road*, 664. Hereafter page numbers are cited in the text.

3. Wright, *Black Boy*, 73. Hereafter page numbers are cited in the text.

4. King, "Letter from Birmingham Jail," 865.

5. James Weldon Johnson, *Autobiography of an Ex-Colored Man*, 19.

6. Quoted in Fabre, *Unfinished Quest of Richard Wright*, 252.

7. Ibid., 252.

8. Mechling, "Failure of Folklore," 291.

9. Quoted in Fabre, *Unfinished Quest of Richard Wright*, 251–52.

10. Cappetti, "Sociology of an Existence," 267.

11. Alice Walker, "Zora Neale Hurston," xvii.

12. Hemenway, *Zora Neale Hurston*, 278.

13. Alice Walker, "Zora Neale Hurston," xvii.

14. Boyd, *Wrapped in Rainbows*, 359.

15. Brantley, *Feminine Sense in Southern Memoir*, 187.

16. Hurston, "How It Feels to Be Colored Me," 153.

17. See Brantley, *Feminine Sense in Southern Memoir*, 188.

18. Hurston, *Their Eyes Were Watching God*, 9.

19. Pierre A. Walker, "Zora Neale Hurston," 387–99.

20. Hemenway, *Zora Neale Hurston*, 286.

21. Domina, "Protection in My Mouf," 197.

22. Gates, " 'Negro Way of Saying,' " 43.

23. Brantley, *Feminine Sense in Southern Memoir*, 215.

24. Hemenway, *Zora Neale Hurston*, 276.

25. Gates, *Colored People*, 35. Hereafter page numbers are cited in the text.

26. Nelson, "Almost Heaven," 794.

27. Middlebrook, "Artful Voyeur," 190.

28. Early, "Speak, Memory," 33–36.

29. Ognibene, review of *Colored People*, 262.

30. See Early, "Speak, Memory"; Nelson, "Almost Heaven"; and Ognibene, review of *Colored People*.

31. Baldwin, *Fire Next Time*, 94.

32. Pinsker, "Home Boys between Hard Covers," 757.

33. Ibid.

34. Early, "Speak, Memory," 33–36.

35. Henry Louis Gates Jr., interview with Brian Lamb, "Booknotes: *Colored People* by Henry Louis Gates, Jr.," first broadcast October 9, 1994, by C-SPAN. Transcript available at www.booknotes.org/Transcript/?ProgramID=1220.

36. Nelson, "Almost Heaven," 794.

37. Mark M. Smith, *How Race Is Made*, 2.

38. Ibid., 3.

39. Ibid., 96.

FOUR. WHITE MEMOIRISTS REMEMBER JIM CROW

1. Morris, *North Toward Home*, 379. Hereafter page numbers are cited in the text.

2. Lillian Smith, *Killers of the Dream*, 91–92. Hereafter page numbers are cited in the text.

3. Hobson, *But Now I See*, 92.

4. Brantley, *Feminine Sense in Southern Memoir*, 51.

5. Loveland, *Lillian Smith*, 11–12; Brantley, *Feminine Sense in Southern Memoir*, 41–42.

6. Gladney, "Personalizing the Political," 93–106.

7. Hobson, *But Now I See*, 33.

8. Loveland, *Lillian Smith*, 70–71.

9. Lillian Smith quoted in ibid., 179.

10. Ibid., 129.

11. Watson, "Uncovering the Body, Discovering Ideology," 477.

12. Ibid., 480–81.

13. William Alexander Percy, *Lanterns on the Levee*, 7. Hereafter page numbers are cited in the text.

14. Romine, *Narrative Forms of Southern Community*, 141.

15. Jenkins, *South in Black and White*, 88–89.

16. See Daniel, *Deep'n As It Come*, and Barry, *Rising Tide*.

17. Full texts of Robert Moton's reports to Herbert Hoover on June 13, 1927, and December 12, 1927, can be found at www.pbs.org/wgbh/amex/flood/filmmore/ps_moton1 .html.

18. See Wyatt-Brown. *House of Percy*.

19. Ibid., 263–70.

20. Walker Percy, introduction, xiii.

21. Wyatt-Brown, *House of Percy*, 267.

22. Many critics have noted the homoerotic overtones of many passages in *Lanterns on the Levee*, including Percy's descriptions of his relationship with Ford. William Armstrong Percy, history professor at the University of Massachusetts, Boston (and a Percy family member), claims that William Alexander Percy and his valet Ford had a sexual relationship. See William Armstrong Percy, "William Alexander Percy."

CONCLUSION

1. Litwack, *Trouble in Mind*, xvi.

2. Ibid., 41.

3. Hall, " 'You Must Remember This,' " 465.

4. Ibid., 464.

5. Wright, *Black Boy*, 206.

6. Hurston, *Dust Tracks on a Road*, 588.

7. Stepto, "Literacy and Ascent," 252.

8. Hakutani, "Creation of the Self," 70.

9. Du Bois, "Richard Wright Looks Back," 2.

10. Ibid.

11. Adams, " 'I Do Believe Him,' " 302.

12. Fabre, *Unfinished Quest of Richard Wright*, 5.

13. Ibid., 46.

14. Bontemps, "From Eatonville, Florida to Harlem."

15. Hemenway, *Zora Neale Hurston*, 276.

16. Boyd, *Wrapped in Rainbows*, 354.

17. Bordelon, "New Tracks on *Dust Tracks*," 11.

18. Boyd, *Wrapped in Rainbows*, 354.

19. Wright, "Between Laugher and Tears," 23.

20. Hurston, review of *Uncle Tom's Children.*
21. Hurston, *Dust Tracks on a Road,* 599.
22. Morris, *North Toward Home,* 195.
23. Ibid., 377.
24. William Alexander Percy, *Lanterns on the Levee,* 24.

BIBLIOGRAPHY

Adams, Timothy Dow. " 'I Do Believe Him Though I Know He Lies': Lying as Genre
    and Metaphor in *Black Boy*." In *Richard Wright: Critical Perspectives Past and
    Present*, edited by Henry Louis Gates Jr. and K. A. Appiah, 302–15. New York:
    Amistad, 1993.
————. *Telling Lies in Modern American Autobiography*. Chapel Hill: University of
    North Carolina Press, 1990.
Anchor, Robert. "Realism and Ideology: The Question of Order." *History and Theory*
    22, no. 2 (1983): 107–19.
Andrews, William L. *African American Autobiography: A Collection of Critical Essays*.
    Englewood Cliffs, N.J.: Prentice Hall, 1993.
Appleby, Joyce, Lynn Hunt, and Margaret Jacob. *Telling the Truth about History*. New
    York: W. W. Norton, 1995.
Attebery, Brian. "American Studies: A Not So Unscientific Method." *American
    Quarterly* 48, no. 2 (1996): 316–43.
Baldwin, James. *The Fire Next Time*. 1961. Reprint, New York: Vintage, 1993.
Barry, John M. *Rising Tide: The Great Mississippi River Flood of 1927 and How It
    Changed America*. New York: Simon and Schuster, 1998.
Barthes, Roland. *Roland Barthes*. New York: Macmillan, 1996.
Barzun, Jacques, and Henry F. Graff. *The Modern Researcher*. 5th ed. Fort Worth, Tex.:
    Harcourt Brace Jovanovich College Publishers, 1992.
Berger, Peter L., and Thomas Luckmann. *The Social Construction of Reality: A Treatise
    in the Sociology of Knowledge*. New York: Doubleday, 1966.
Berry, J. Bill. "Class Southerner." In *Located Lives: Place and Idea in Southern
    Autobiography*, edited by J. Bill Berry, 167–87. Athens: University of Georgia
    Press, 1990.
Billson, Marcus. "The Memoir: New Perspectives on a Forgotten Genre." *Genre* 10,
    no. 2 (1977): 259–82.
Blassingame, John. "Black Autobiographies as History and Literature." *Black Scholar*
    5 (1974): 2–7.
Blight, David W. "W. E. B. Du Bois and the Struggle for American Historical
    Memory." In *History and Memory in African-American Culture*, edited by
    Genevieve Fabre and Robert O'Meally, 45–71. Oxford: Oxford University Press,
    1994.

Bontemps, Arna. "From Eatonville, Florida to Harlem." *New York Herald Tribune*, November 22, 1942.

Bordelon, Pam. "New Tracks on *Dust Tracks*: Toward a Reassessment of the Life of Zora Neale Hurston." *African American Review* 31, no. 1 (1997): 5–21.

Boyd, Valerie. *Wrapped in Rainbows: The Life of Zora Neale Hurston*. New York: Scribner, 2003.

Brantley, Will. *Feminine Sense in Southern Memoir*. Jackson: University Press of Mississippi, 1993.

Briggs, Carolyn S. *This Dark World: A Memoir of Salvation Found and Lost*. New York: Bloomsbury, 2002.

Bruss, Elizabeth. *Autobiographical Acts: The Changing Situation of a Literary Genre*. Baltimore: Johns Hopkins University Press, 1976.

Burke, Peter. *New Perspectives on Historical Writing*. University Park: Pennsylvania State University Press, 1991.

Canary, Robert H., and Henry Kozicki, eds. *The Writing of History: Literary Form and Historical Understanding*. Madison: University of Wisconsin Press, 1978.

Cappetti, Carla. "Sociology of an Existence: Wright and the Chicago School." In *Richard Wright: Critical Perspectives Past and Present*, edited by Henry Louis Gates Jr. and K. A. Appiah, 255–71. New York: Amistad, 1993.

Clark, G. Kitson. *The Critical Historian*. London: Heinemann, 1967.

Clifford, James. "On Ethnographic Allegory." In *Writing Culture: The Poetics and Politics of Ethnography*, edited by James Clifford and George E. Marcus, 98–121. Berkeley: University of California Press, 1986.

Cobb, James C. *The Most Southern Place on Earth: The Mississippi Delta and the Roots of Regional Identity*. New York: Oxford University Press, 1992.

Collin, Finn. *Social Reality*. London: Routledge, 1997.

Collingwood, R. G. *The Idea of History*. Oxford: Oxford University Press, 1946.

Confino, Michael. "Some Random Thoughts on History's Recent Past." *History and Memory* 12, no. 2 (2001): 29–57.

Cox, James. *Recovering Literature's Lost Ground: Essays in American Autobiography*. Baton Rouge: Louisiana State University Press, 1989.

Crews, Harry. *A Childhood: The Biography of a Place*. New York: Quill, 1983.

Daniel, Pete. *Deep'n As It Come: The 1927 Mississippi River Flood*. New York: Oxford University Press, 1993.

De Man, Paul. "Autobiography as De-facement." *Modern Language Notes* 97, no. 5 (1979): 919–30.

Dilthey, Wilhelm. *Pattern and Meaning in History*. Edited by H. P. Rickman. New York: Harper and Row, 1961.

Domina, Lynn. "Protection in My Mouf: Self, Voice, and Community in Zora Neale Hurston's *Dust Tracks on a Road* and *Mules and Men*." *African American Review* 31, no. 2 (1997): 197–209.

Du Bois, W. E. B. *Black Reconstruction in America: 1860–1880*. 1935. Reprint, New York: Touchstone, 1995.

————. "Richard Wright Looks Back." Review of *Black Boy* by Richard Wright, *New York Herald Tribune Book Review*, March 4, 1945, 2.

Eagleton, Terry. *Literary Theory: An Introduction*. 2nd ed. Minneapolis: University of Minnesota Press, 1996.

Eakin, Paul John. *Touching the World: Reference in Autobiography*. Princeton, N.J.: Princeton University Press, 1992.

Early, Gerald. "Speak, Memory." *New Republic*, July 4, 1994, 33–36.

Egan, Susanna. *Mirror Talk*. Chapel Hill: University of North Carolina Press, 1999.

Elton, G. R. *Return to Essentials: Some Reflections on the Present State of Historical Study*. Cambridge: Cambridge University Press, 1991.

Fabre, Michel. *The Unfinished Quest of Richard Wright*. Urbana: University of Illinois Press, 1993.

Fields, Karen. "What One Cannot Remember Mistakenly." In *History and Memory in African-American Culture*, edited by Genevieve Fabre and Robert O'Meally, 150–63. Oxford: Oxford University Press, 1994.

Foucault, Michel. "Nietzsche, Genealogy, History." In *Language, Counter-Memory, Practice*, edited by Donald F. Bouchard, 139–64. Ithaca, N.Y.: Cornell University Press, 1977.

Franke, William. "Metaphor and the Making of Sense: The Contemporary Metaphor Renaissance." *Philosophy and Rhetoric* 33, no. 2 (2000): 137–53.

Gates, Henry Louis, Jr. *Colored People*. New York: Vintage, 1995.

————. "'A Negro Way of Saying.'" Review of *Dust Tracks on a Road* and *Moses: Man of the Mountain*, by Zora Neale Hurston, *New York Times Book Review*, April 21, 1985, 43.

Geertz, Clifford, ed. *Writing Culture: The Poetics and Politics of Ethnography*. Berkeley: University of California Press, 1986.

Gibbs, Raymond W. "When Is Metaphor? The Idea of Understanding in Theories of Metaphor." *Poetics Today* 13, no. 4 (1992): 575–606.

Gladney, Margaret Rose. "Personalizing the Political, Politicizing the Personal: Reflections on Editing the Letters of Lillian Smith." In *Carryin' On in the Lesbian and Gay South*, edited by John Howard, 93–106. New York: New York University, 1997.

Gorra, Michael. "The Autobiographical Turn." *Transition*, no. 68 (1995): 143–53.

Gusdorf, Georges. "Conditions and Limits of Autobiography." In *Autobiography: Essays Theoretical and Critical*, edited by James Olney, 28–48. Princeton, N.J.: Princeton University Press, 1980.

Hakutani, Yoshinobu. "Creation of the Self in Richard Wright's *Black Boy*." *Black American Literature Forum* 10, no. 2 (1985): 70–75.

Hall, Jacquelyn Dowd. "'You Must Remember This': Autobiography as Social Critique." *Journal of American History* 85, no. 2 (1998): 439–65.

Harlan, David. "Intellectual History and the Return of Literature." *American Historical Review* 94 (1989): 581–609.

Hemenway, Robert. *Zora Neale Hurston: A Literary Biography*. Urbana: University of Illinois Press, 1977.

Hirsch, E. D., Jr. "Transhistorical Intentions and the Persistence of Allegory." *New Literary History* 25, no. 3 (1994): 549–67.

Hobson, Fred. *But Now I See: The White Southern Racial Conversion Narrative*. Baton Rouge: Louisiana State University Press, 1999.

Howarth, William. "Writing Upside Down: Voice and Place in Southern Autobiography." In *Located Lives: Place and Idea in Southern Autobiography*, edited by J. Bill Berry, 3–19. Athens: University of Georgia Press, 1990.

Hurston, Zora Neale. *Dust Tracks on a Road*. In *Hurston: Folklore, Memoirs, and Other Writing*. New York: Library of America, 1995.

———. "How It Feels to Be Colored Me." In *I Love Myself When I Am Laughing . . . A Zora Neale Hurston Reader*, edited by Alice Walker, 152–55. Westbury, N.Y.: Feminist Press, 1979.

———. Review of *Uncle Tom's Children* by Richard Wright. *Saturday Review of Literature*, April 2, 1938.

———. *Their Eyes Were Watching God*. Urbana: University of Illinois Press, 1978.

Iacocca, Lee, and William Novak. *Lee Iacocca: An Autobiography*. New York: Bantam Books, 1986.

Inscoe, John C. "Black, White, and Southern: Autobiography and the Complexities of Race." Georgia Humanities Lecture, May 12, 2005, Atlanta.

Jenkins, McKay. *The South in Black and White: Race, Sex, and Literature in the 1940s*. Chapel Hill: University of North Carolina Press, 1999.

Johnson, Barbara. "Thresholds of Difference: Structures of Address in Zora Neale Hurston." In *"Race," Writing, and Difference*, edited by Henry Louis Gates Jr., 317–28. Chicago: University of Chicago Press, 1986.

Johnson, James Weldon. *Autobiography of an Ex-Colored Man*. New York: Hill and Wang, 1960.

Kadar, Marlene. *Essays on Life Writing: From Genre to Critical Practice*. Toronto: University of Toronto Press, 1992.

King, Martin Luther, Jr. "Letter from Birmingham Jail (1963)." Reprinted in *Black Writers of America: A Contemporary Anthology*, edited by Richard Barksdale and Keneth Kinnamon, 863–71. New York: Macmillan, 1972.

Kundera, Milan. *The Book of Laughter and Forgetting*. Translated by Michael Henry Heim. New York: Knopf, 1981.

Leibowitz, Herbert. *Fabricating Lives: Explorations in American Autobiography*. New York: Knopf, 1989.

Lejeune, Philippe. *On Autobiography*. Minneapolis: University of Minnesota Press, 1989.

Levinson, Jerrold. "Intention and Interpretation: A Last Look." In *Intention and Interpretation*, edited by Gary Iseminger, 221–56. Philadelphia: Temple University Press, 1995.

Litwack, Leon. *Trouble in Mind: Black Southerners in the Age of Jim Crow*. Knopf: New York, 1998.

Livingston, Paisley. "Intentionalism in Aesthetics." *New Literary History* 29, no. 4 (1998): 831–46.

Lorenz, Chris. "Historical Knowledge and Historical Reality: A Plea for 'Internal Realism.'" *History and Theory* 33, no. 3 (1994): 297–328.

Loveland, Anne C. *Lillian Smith: A Southerner Confronting the South.* Baton Rouge: Louisiana State University Press, 1986.

Mahan, William. *Behind the Burnt Cork Mask: Early Blackface Minstrelsy and Antebellum American Popular Culture.* Urbana: University of Illinois, 1998.

Marcus, Laura. *Auto/biographical Discourses: Theory, Criticism, Practice.* Manchester, England: Manchester University Press, 1994.

Mechling, Jay. "The Failure of Folklore in Richard Wright's *Black Boy.*" *Journal of American Folklore* 103, no. 413 (1991): 274–94.

Megill, Allan. "The Reception of Foucault by Historians." *Journal of the History of Ideas* 48, no. 1 (1987): 117–41.

Middlebrook, Diane. "The Artful Voyeur: Anna Deavere Smith and Henry Louis Gates, Jr. on Private Life and Public Art." *Transition* 67 (1995): 187–97.

Miller, Nancy K. "But Enough about Me, What Do You Think of My Memoir?" *Yale Journal of Criticism* 13, no. 2 (2000): 421–36.

Morris, Willie. *North Toward Home.* New York: Dell, 1967.

Nabokov, Vladimir. *Speak, Memory.* New York: G. P. Putnam's Sons, 1966.

Nagel, Thomas. *The View from Nowhere.* Oxford: Oxford University Press, 1986.

Nelson, Jill. "Almost Heaven." *The Nation*, June 6, 1994, 794–97.

Nora, Pierre. "Between Memory and History: *Les Lieux de Memoire.*" *Representations*, no. 26 (1989): 7–24.

Novick, Peter. *That Noble Dream: The "Objectivity Question" and the American Historical Profession.* Cambridge: Cambridge University Press, 1988.

Nowell-Smith, P. H. "The Constructionist Theory of History." *History and Theory* 16, no. 4 (1977): 1–28.

Ognibene, Elaine R. Review of *Colored People* by Henry Louis Gates Jr. *Journal of Men's Studies* 3, no. 3 (1995): 262.

Olney, James. "(Auto)biography." *Southern Review* 22 (1986): 428–41.

———, ed. *Autobiography: Essays Theoretical and Critical.* Princeton, N.J.: Princeton University Press, 1980.

———. *Studies in Autobiography.* New York: Oxford University Press, 1988.

O'Meally, Robert. "On Burke and the Vernacular: Ralph Ellison's Boomerang of History." In *History and Memory in African-American Culture*, edited by Genevieve Fabre and Robert O'Meally, 244–60. Oxford: Oxford University Press, 1994.

Pascal, Roy. *Design and Truth in Autobiography.* Cambridge: Harvard University Press, 1960.

Percy, Walker. Introduction to *Lanterns on the Levee: Recollections of a Planter's Son*, by William Alexander Percy. Baton Rouge: Louisiana State University Press, 1994.

Percy, William Alexander. *Lanterns on the Levee: Recollections of a Planter's Son.* 1941. Reprint, Baton Rouge: Louisiana State University Press, 1994.

Percy, William Armstrong. "William Alexander Percy (1885–1942): His Homosexuality and Why It Matters." In *Carryin' On in the Lesbian and Gay South*, edited by John Howard, 75–92. New York: New York University Press, 1997.

Pinsker, Sanford. "Home Boys between Hard Covers." *Virginia Quarterly Review* 70, no. 4 (1994): 757–73.

Pocock, J. G. A. *Virtue, Commerce, and History: Essays on Political Thought and History, Chiefly in the Eighteenth Century.* Cambridge: Cambridge University Press, 1985.

Popkin, Jeremy D. "Historians on the Autobiographical Frontier." *American Historical Review* 104, no. 3 (1999): 725–48.

————. *History, Historians, and Autobiography.* Chicago: University of Chicago Press, 2005.

Prins, Gwyn. "Oral History." In *New Perspectives in Historical Writing,* edited by Peter Burke, 114–39. University Park: Pennsylvania State University Press, 1991.

Putnam, Hilary. *Reason, Truth, and History.* Cambridge: Cambridge University Press, 1981.

Romine, Scott. *The Narrative Forms of Southern Community.* Baton Rouge: Louisiana State University Press, 1999.

Rowley, Hazel. *Richard Wright: The Life and Times.* New York: Henry Holt, 2001.

Said, Edward. "Invention, Memory, Place." *Critical Inquiry* 26, no. 2 (2000): 175–92.

Sayre, Robert F. "The Proper Study—Autobiographies in American Studies." *American Quarterly* 29, no. 3 (1977): 241–62.

Shen, Yeshayahu. "Cognitive Aspects of Metaphor Comprehension: An Introduction." *Poetics Today* 13, no. 4 (1992): 567–74.

Shiner, Larry. "Reading Foucault: Anti-Method and the Genealogy of Power-Knowledge." *History and Theory* 21, no. 3 (1982): 382–99.

Smith, Lillian. *Killers of the Dream.* 1949. Reprint, New York: W. W. Norton, 1994.

Smith, Mark M. *How Race Is Made: Slavery, Segregation, and the Senses.* Chapel Hill: University of North Carolina Press, 2006.

Smith, Sidonie, and Julie Watson. *Reading Autobiography: A Guide for Interpreting Life Narrative.* Minneapolis: University of Minnesota Press, 2001.

Stanford, Michael. *Introduction to the Philosophy of History.* Oxford: Blackwell Publishers, 1998.

Stearns, Peter N., and Jan Lewis. *An Emotional History of the United States.* New York: New York University Press, 1998.

Stepto, Robert. "Literacy and Ascent: *Black Boy.*" In *Richard Wright: Critical Perspectives Past and Present,* edited by Henry Louis Gates Jr. and K. A. Appiah, 226–54. New York: Amistad, 1993.

Stern, Fritz, ed. *The Varieties of History: From Voltaire to the Present.* New York: Meridian Books, 1956.

Stockley, David. "Empathetic Reconstruction in History and History Teaching." *History and Theory* 22, no. 4 (1983): 50–65.

Stone, Albert. *Autobiographical Occasions and Original Acts: Versions of American Identity from Henry Adams to Nate Shaw.* Philadelphia: University of Pennsylvania Press, 1982.

Thelan, David. "Memory and American History." *Journal of American History* 75, no. 4 (1989): 1117–29.

Thompson, Paul. *The Voice of the Past: Oral History.* Oxford: Oxford University Press, 2000.

Walker, Alice. "Zora Neale Hurston—a Cautionary Tale and a Partisan View." In *Zora Neale Hurston: A Literary Biography*, Robert Hemenway, xi–xx. Urbana: University of Illinois Press, 1977.

Walker, Margaret. *Richard Wright: Daemonic Genius.* New York: Amistad, 1988.

Walker, Pierre A. "Zora Neale Hurston and the Post-modern Self in *Dust Tracks on a Road*." *African American Review* 32, no. 3 (1998): 387–99.

Watson, Jay. "Uncovering the Body, Discovering Ideology: Segregation and Sexual Anxiety in Lillian Smith's *Killers of the Dream*." *American Quarterly* 49, no. 3 (1997): 470–503.

Welty, Eudora. "Must the Novelist Crusade?" In *The Eye of the Story: Selected Essays and Reviews.* New York: Vintage, 1990.

———. "Place in Fiction." *South Atlantic Quarterly* 55 (1956): 62.

White, Luise. "Telling More: Lies, Secrets, and History." *History and Theory* 39, no. 4 (2000): 11–22.

Wimsatt, W. M. *The Verbal Icon: Studies in the Meaning of Poetry.* New York: Noonday Press, 1966.

Windschuttle, Keith. *The Killing of History: How Literary Critics and Social Theorists Are Murdering Our Past.* New York: Free Press, 1996.

Wolff, Robert Paul. *Moneybags Must Be So Lucky: On the Literary Structure of Capital.* Amherst: University of Massachusetts Press, 1988.

———. "Narrative Time: The Inherently Perspectival Structure of the Human World." *Midwest Studies in Philosophy* 15 (1990): 210–23.

Wright, Richard. "Between Laugher and Tears." *New Masses*, October 5, 1937, 22–23.

———. *Black Boy (American Hunger).* Restored text. New York: Harper Perennial, 1998.

Wyatt-Brown, Bertram. *The House of Percy: Honor, Melancholy, and Imagination in a Southern Family.* New York: Oxford University Press, 1994.

Zinsser, William, ed. *Inventing the Truth: The Art and Craft of Memoir.* Boston: Houghton Mifflin, 1998.

INDEX

Adams, Timothy Dow, 31, 142
agency, historical, 22
allegory, 48–49
ambivalence, in Jim Crow autobiography, 139–40
Anchor, Robert, 22, 23
Anderson, Linda, 6
Angelou, Maya, 54
antebellum South, 124, 128–29, 149
anthropology, 5, 72, 83
Appleby, Joyce, 22
Arkansas, 1, 2, 53, 58, 69, 129, 141, 146
Attebery, Brian, 26
autobiography studies, 6–7

Baldwin, James, 88, 91, 93
Barthes, Roland, 19
Barzun, Jacques, 26, 40
Berger, Peter, 28
Berry, J. Bill, 53–54
Black Boy (Wright), 57–72, 137; allegory and, 48–49; author's encounter with, 1–4; Book of the Month Club and, 71; compared with *Dust Tracks on a Road*, 73; descriptions of rural landscape and, 60–62; "ethics of Jim Crow" and, 66; Great Migration and, 68; hunger and, 62–65; individual versus group identity in, 71–72; irony and, 65–69; metaphor and, 42–44, 64–65; psychological damage of racism and, 69–70; reviews of, 142; mentioned,

9, 11, 57, 73, 100, 106, 139, 140, 142, 147
black community: Gates and, 94; Hurston and, 82, 85; Morris and, 104; Percy, W. A., and, 127–28; Wright and, 69–71
Blight, David, 33, 40
Bloom, Harold, 78
Boas, Franz, 83
Bontemps, Arna, 143
Bordelon, Pam, 144
Boyd, Valerie, 74, 143, 144
Brantley, Will, 74, 84, 113
Briggs, Carolyn, 44–45

Cappetti, Carla, 71
Chicago, 70
Chicago Defender, 132
civil rights movement: *Brown* decision and, 92, 107, 108; Gates and, 92, 95–96, 98, 99, 136; legislation and, 10; March on Montgomery and, 46; Morris and, 99; National Association for the Advancement of Colored People (NAACP) and, 108; school desegregation and, 108; Student Nonviolent Coordinating Committee (SNCC) and, 102, 112, 153; mentioned, 75, 76, 100, 152, 153. *See also* King, Martin Luther, Jr.
Civil War, 102
Clifford, James, 48–49

Collin, Finn, 28
Collingwood, R. G., 23–25, 26, 37, 59
Colored People (Gates), 86–98; compared
    with *Black Boy*, 87–88; compared
    with *Dust Tracks on a Road*, 87–88,
    92–93; irony and, 95–96; nostalgia
    and, 86–87, 91, 92, 94, 152, 153;
    reviews of, 88; sense impressions
    and, 97–98; mentioned, 11, 57,
    100
Confino, Michael, 20
conservatives, 118
Crews, Harry, 32, 53

Davis, Jefferson, 101
Derrida, Jacques, 19
Dilthey, Wilhelm, 23, 25
disciplinary proprietorship of autobiog-
    raphy, 5–6, 7–8
Domina, Lynn, 82
Douglass, Frederick, 150
Du Bois, W. E. B., 16, 40, 142
Dunning School, 16
Dust Tracks on a Road (Hurston), 72–86;
    audience for, 73, 76–77; critiques of,
    73; discussions of racism and, 75–77;
    folktales and, 82–84; irony and,
    80–83; reviews of, 143; mentioned, 11,
    57, 100, 140, 142, 147

Eagleton, Terry, 37, 39, 41
Eakin, Paul John, 7, 19, 20
Early, Gerald, 91
Egan, Susanna, 36
Ellison, Ralph, 88
Elton, Geoffrey, 18
emotions, 25–28; *Black Boy* and, 141; *Dust
    Tracks on a Road* and, 141; emotional
    truth and, 5; felt experience and, 3,
    12, 59, 67, 80, 100, 103, 106, 125, 138,
    139, 140, 148; historical understanding
    and, 21, 25, 26–27, 36; refeeling
    and, 26, 27, 49, 71; Wright and, 58;

mentioned, 7, 9, 12, 15, 21, 36, 145,
    148, 154
empathy, 3, 9, 150; empathetic
    reconstruction, 26–28, 37, 125
ethnography, 48–49

Fabre, Michel, 142
falsehoods. *See* lying.
Faulkner, William, 53
feelings. *See* emotions
felt experience. *See* emotions
fiction, 9, 49, 50, 55
Fields, Karen, 33
Florida, 73, 113, 141, 146; Eatonville, 77,
    143, 147; Jacksonville, 77
folklore, 41, 48; Gates and, 88; Hurston
    and, 82–84; Wright and, 70
Foote, Henry S., 101, 102
Foucault, Michel, 19, 20
Franke, William, 41
Fugitive poets, 113

Gates, Henry Louis, Jr., 85–86; analysis
    by, of *Dust Tracks on a Road*, 84;
    career of, 87, 89; compared with
    Hurston, 89; compared with Morris,
    151–53; education of, 90; father of, 90;
    Maggie, daughter of, 89–90, 93–94;
    mother of, 98; nostalgia and, 140;
    uncle of, 90, 91; mentioned, 11, 57.
    See also *Colored People*
genre, 5, 6, 8–9, 17
geographical spaces, 53–55, 99–100, 103
Georgia, 114
Gibbs, Raymond, 42
Graff, Henry F., 26, 40
Great Depression, 74
Great Migration, 68
Gusdorf, Georges, 6

Hakutani, Yoshinobu, 142
Hall, Jacquelyn Dowd, 137, 139
Harlan, David, 51

Harlem Renaissance, 73

Harper's, 99, 109

Hemenway, Robert, 73, 82, 84, 143, 144

Hirsch, E. D., 48

historians, 51–52; belief in a knowable past and, 20; as scientists, 3. *See also* history

historical agents (subjects): autobiographers as, 22; as representative, 13; subjectivity of, 15, 23; thoughts of, 24, 25; mentioned, 5, 17, 21, 22

historical imagination, 26

historical memory, 31–32; construction of, 32–33; imagination and, 32; memory palaces and, 40–41; present significance of, 33–34; mentioned, 144

historiography, 16, 149

history, 15, 138; as distinct from literary studies, 18, 19; historical perspective and, 19; methods and, 7–8; as multiperspectival, 15–16; professionalization of, 5, 6, 14; as science, 6; theory and, 23; as vicarious experience, 26, 27, 40

Hobson, Fred, 107, 108, 115

Howard University, 76

Howarth, William, 53

Hunt, Lynn, 22

Hurston, Zora Neale, 72–86; Barnard College and, 73, 83, 89; biographical information on, 141; birthplace of, 143; compared with Wright, 141–48; father of, 78–79, 146; grandfather of, 79; mother of, 146; racial awakening and, 77–78; response of, to segregation, 74; review by, of *Uncle Tom's Children*, 146; mentioned, 11, 57, 94, 98, 139, 147

—works: *Jonah's Gourd Vine*, 73, 74; *Their Eyes Were Watching God*, 73, 78, 146. See also *Dust Tracks on a Road*

Iacocca, Lee, 37, 38, 39

intentionalism, 8–9

irony, 44–48, 65–69, 80–83, 96–97; definition of, 44; mentioned, 36, 47, 55

Jacob, Margaret, 22

Jenkins, McKay, 128

Jim Crow: character of, 10–11; definition of, 10–11, 75

Johnson, James Weldon, 67

Jolly, Margaretta, 7

Jonah's Gourd Vine (Hurston), 73, 74

Killers of the Dream (L. Smith), 113–23; Janie episode and, 123; metaphor and, 122; psychological damage of racism to whites described in, 115–16, 118; segregation and the body in, 122; stereotyped descriptions of African Americans in, 51–52, 118–20; white women discussed in, 116–17; mentioned, 11, 51, 151

King, Martin Luther, Jr., 46, 47, 67, 89, 92, 95

Kundera, Milan, 34

language: conceptual, 51–52; problems of, 19–20

Lanterns on the Levee (W. A. Percy), 123–35; compared with *Black Boy*, 128; compared with *Killers of the Dream*, 125, 127; description of whites as victims in, 124–25, 150; southern identity and, 125–27; stereotypes of African Americans in, 127–28; mentioned, 12, 151

Leibowitz, Herbert, 5

Lejeune, Philippe, 8

Levinson, Jerrold, 9

Lewis, Jan, 12, 25

liberals and liberalism, 111, 112, 117, 118, 143

Lippincott, Bertram, 73
literary techniques, 50–51; allegory,
    48–49; literary compared with
    nonliterary language, 36–40, 41;
    symbols, 55; mentioned, 4, 5, 10, 25,
    35, 36, 39, 55, 59, 106. See also *Black
    Boy*; *Colored People*; *Dust Tracks on
    a Road*; irony; *Killers of the Dream*;
    Lanterns on the Levee; metaphor;
    North Toward Home
literature, 18, 138; as art, 6; autobiography
    as, 5; feared encroachment of, on
    history, 18; literary perspective of, 19
Litwack, Leon, 136–37
Livingston, Paisley, 8
Lorenz, Chris, 21
Louisiana, 129
Luckmann, Thomas, 28
lying, 9, 30, 31, 144–45; *Black Boy* and,
    140, 142–43, 145; *Dust Tracks on a
    Road* and, 140, 143–44, 145
lynching, 10, 70, 149

Mechling, Jay, 70
memoir, 5
memory. *See* historical memory
Mencken, H. L., 53
metaphor, 41–44, 64–65; mentioned, 36,
    54, 55, 122. See also *Black Boy*; *Dust
    Tracks on a Road*; *Killers of the Dream*
minstrel acts, 11
Mississippi, 53, 140, 141, 146; Delta, 2, 86,
    103, 129, 154; differing descriptions of,
    99–100, 136, 153–54; Greenville, 133;
    Morris and, 46, 104, 106, 108, 109;
    Natchez, 59; University of Mississippi,
    107; Wright and, 1, 58, 60–62, 69, 70
Mississippi River Flood of 1927, 129–33
Morris, Willie, 99–100, 101–12; compared
    with Gates, 151–53; correspondence
    with Wright, 112; Foote (ancestor)
    and, 101, 102; *Harpers* and, 99,
    109; John Birch Society and, 107;

literary art and, 106; *New York
    Days*, 110; nostalgia and, 152, 153;
    Rhodes fellowship and, 107, 151; *Texas
    Observer* and, 107; mentioned, 11, 46,
    53, 120, 121, 123, 136, 140, 146. See also
    North Toward Home
Moton, Robert, 132

Nabokov, Vladimir, 37, 38–39
Nagel, Thomas, 15
Native Son (Wright), 87
Nelson, Jill, 88, 96
New York, 46, 99, 103, 109, 113, 141
New York Days (Morris), 110
Nora, Pierre, 31, 32
North Toward Home (Morris), 99–100,
    101–12; ambivalence in, 104–6; irony
    and, 46–47; racial epithets and, 103;
    mentioned, 11
Novick, Peter, 17
Nowell-Smith, P. H., 21

objectivity, 3–4, 13–18; correspondence
    with past and, 17; emotions and,
    26; limitations of, 15; literary critics
    and, 18–19; possibility of, 13–14, 18;
    professionalized history and, 14; truth
    and, 3; as "value neutral," 16–17, 26;
    mentioned, 9, 23, 27
Ognibene, Elaine, 91
Olney, James, 5
O'Meally, Robert, 40
oral history, 14, 30, 31, 83

participant-observers, 5, 72
Percy, LeRoy, 124, 130
Percy, Walker, 134
Percy, William Alexander, 123–35;
    compared with Smith, L., 149–51;
    Ford (servant) and, 133–34, 135; LeRoy
    Percy (father) and, 124, 130; noblesse
    oblige and, 124, 127, 130, 131, 135;
    Red Cross involvement with, 129–33;

Walker Percy (nephew) and, 134; mentioned, 12, 53, 100, 101, 118, 119, 123, 140, 154. See also *Lanterns on the Levee*

Welty, Eudora, 53, 74
West Virginia Piedmont, 86, 89, 90, 94, 95, 96
White, Hayden, 30
White, Luise, 31
White Citizens Council, 108
Windschuttle, Keith, 18
Wolff, Robert Paul, 28, 29, 45–46
Woodward, C. Vann, 46, 47
Wright, Richard, 1–4, 57–72; biographical information on, 141; black community and, 71; compared with Hurston, 141–48; correspondence with Morris, 112; father of, 62, 69, 146; feelings and, 58, 59, 64; grandmother of, 64, 70; Griggs (friend) and, 67, 68; literary techniques and, 59, 62; mother of, 62, 70, 146; protest tradition and, 93; review by, of *Their Eyes Were Watching God*, 146; Wall family and, 142–43; mentioned, 11, 77, 84, 85, 86, 98, 120, 128, 133, 137, 139, 147, 154
—works: *Native Son*, 87; *Uncle Tom's Children*, 146. See also *Black Boy*
Wyatt-Brown, Bertram, 132, 134